PocheCouleur

Translated from the French by

Geoffrey Finch, Ellen Krabbe and Kirk McElhearn

Art director
Ahmed-Chaouki Rafif
Assistant
Marie-Pierre Kerbrat

Printed in France

THE LOUVRE

A Palace,
A Museum...

Jean-Jacques Lévêque

ACR Edition

PocheCouleur

The Louvre *(illustration by Philippe Biard, Guides Gallimard Louvre, Edition Nouveaux Loisirs).*
In its final development, the Louvre extended its branches westward in the direction of the growth of the city of Paris, of which it was the strategic and symbolic center. At the center of the Cour Napoleon, the Pyramid presents a new way of approaching it, through its lower levels. The intense activity underground with the many shops, prepares one for the visit. This contributes to the warm and friendly atmosphere that inspires both a visit to the Louvre, as well as the way one approaches the works of art. They are in this way closely associated with daily life.

demands of a clientele concerned with resemblance to the model, their presentation to their best advantage, and the view of refined and rustic surroundings loved by this society enthusiastic for the art of gardening. The subtly concentrated light plays with the silken brilliance of the garments and the delicate complexion of the model. In its conventional style, he prefigures the dark secrets of the undercurrents of Romanticism.

Photo Credits

Archives ACR-JJL. DR. Guides Gallimard, Editions Nouveaux Loisirs, p. 5. Hoa Qui/Alfred Wolf, Paris, pp. 60, 61. RMN, Paris, pp. 32, 35, 49, 53, 66. RMN/Caroline Rose, Paris, pp. 8, 25, 26, 27, 29, 33. RMN/C. Jean, Paris, pp. 54, 64. RMN/D. Arnaudet, Paris, pp. 28, 36. RMN/Gérard Blot-C. Jean, Paris, pp. 34, 37. RMN/Gérard Blot, Paris, pp. 12, 19, 20, 47, 51, 57, 63, 69. RMN/J.L'Hoir, Paris, p. 67. RMN/ M. Bellot, Paris, p. 15. RMN/Beck-Coppola, Paris, p. 39. RMN/ Ropovitch, Paris, p. 11. RMN/R.G. Ojeda-El Majd, Paris, p. 45.

Contents

From Wolves to Kings

*A*ccording to legend, the site of the Louvre was long ago infested with wolves. A slight phonetic change, and the French word 'loup', meaning wolf, gave birth to the name that would be used for a palace, and eventually, a museum. But first it was a fortress.

As Paris became the capital of France, its nascent monarchy wanted to provide it with monuments that would also ensure its defense. The Louvre began as part of a much larger defense program integrated into the Philip Augustus city wall. Vestiges of this wall can still be seen in different places around Paris. But the Louvre was the heart of this defensive structure, just as the Bastille became the heart of the later Charles V wall.

An imposing fortress was built in the beginning of the 13th century. At first, it was a collection of walls surrounding a sturdy dungeon, whose foundations can still be seen, and whose role was much more defensive than residential. The king was living in his palace on the Ile de la Cité (today the Palais de Justice - the Law Courts), in Vincennes, or in the Hôtel Saint-Pol. But it was the Louvre that was the real sign of his power. Its tower contained the royal archives, his treasure, and, from the time of Charles V, a library, that was the foundation for the National Library. Many important prisoners were also detained there.

But for a long while, the kings of France preferred other palaces, until François I put all his energy into building the chateaux in the Loire valley and Fontainebleau, his favorite residence.

Important changes affected the original building as it

progressively lost its defensive function to become an expression of royal wealth, illustrating the profound changes that the representation of power can bring about. At first the palace shared its space with military power, then added luxury, and, as time went on, looked to art for its credibility.

With its crenellated walls, its towers and turrets, and the weather vanes and pennants wafting in the wind, the overall impression of the Louvre on the urban landscape was regal. It is the image we see in the bright and detailed paintings of the *Très Riches Heures du Duc de Berry*, by the Limbourg brothers.

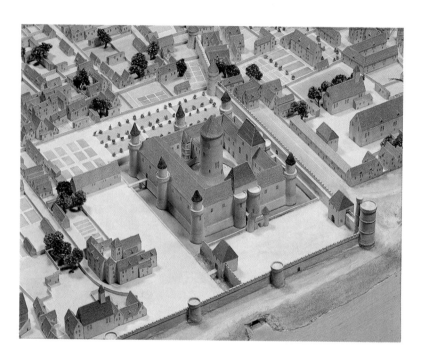

The Louvre in 1380. *Musée du Louvre, Paris.*
It was in 1190 that Philippe Auguste began construction of the keep and castle fortress of the Louvre. At that time, it was nothing more than an outpost of the wall surrounding Paris. The palace on the Ile de la Cité remained the official residence of the king. In 1230, Louis IX, also known as Saint Louis, built the

Grande Salle of the castle (some pillars of the lower room still exist). It was not until 1360-1370 that Charles V built a new wall around Paris (visible today from the shopping galleries of the Louvre) near the Jardin du Carrousel. His architect, Raymond du Temple, enlarged the Louvre by constructing new lodgings as well as redecorating the parts that already existed.

The entire history of the Louvre is marked by its role as a museum, which led to its sumptuous decoration and its vast development. François I, one of its first inhabitants, realized that the Louvre should display his glory and bear witness to his power. It also had to be in the style of the time - the splendor of the Renaissance. He had Pierre Lescot draw up plans around a square courtyard that was one fourth as large as the one we know today. All that came from these extensive plans was one wing, and this was finished under Henri II. This is the section at the southwest corner of what is now known as the Cour

Maître de Saint-Germain-des-Prés.
Piéta (detail). *Musée du Louvre, Paris. This painting offers an exceptional view of the development of the Louvre, along the Seine, with the nearby Hôtel du Petit-Bourbon that would later be absorbed by the enlargement of the Cour Carrée. On the horizon one can see the hill of*

Montmartre crowned with its abbey, and, in the foreground, the abbey of Saint-Germain-des-Prés in its entirety. This view allows one to better appreciate the strategic position of the Louvre in relation to the other highlights of the Parisian cityscape.

Carrée, and that was decorated in part by Jean Goujon. The descendants of the Valois family added the southern wing, and Catherine de Medicis herself had the Petite Galerie, on the banks of the Seine, built by Pierre Lescot.

Having withdrawn to the Louvre and the newly completed Tuileries Palace, the court (Catherine de Medicis and her children) acted as catalysts to lead this complex of buildings to adapt to its new functions. The fortress was progressively replaced by buildings whose elegance were a more appropriate expression of the rituals of court life. This was the beginning of the Louvre as we know it.

Now that the Louvre was completely integrated into the life of the monarchy, it was to live some of the most tragic moments of its history. Those of the Saint-Barthelemy massacre, when royal wealth was sullied by the blood of a massacre.

Having inherited the throne, Henri IV lengthened the Grand Galerie in the direction of the Tuileries, and part of this work is attributed to Jacques Androuet de Cerceau.

Louis XIII had Lemercier double the Pierre Lescot wing. Separated from this by the imposing Pavillon de l'Horloge (also known as the Sully Pavilion), the Cour Carrée now attained its final size. Louis XIV entrusted the completion of this to Le Vau, and gave Claude Perrault (selected over Bernini) the responsibility for the elegant and monumental development of the Colonnade, which completed the Louvre on its eastern side.

The Louvre then expanded toward the west, in the direction of the Tuileries, which seemed to exercise an irresistible attraction, as though the dream of a "Grand Louvre" existed even then, a dream that was only recently realized.

At the same time, the court moved to Versailles, following Louis XIV, leaving the palace to the various administrations grouped there: the Royal Mint, the Royal Printing Press, and, up until 1671, the tapestry workshops.

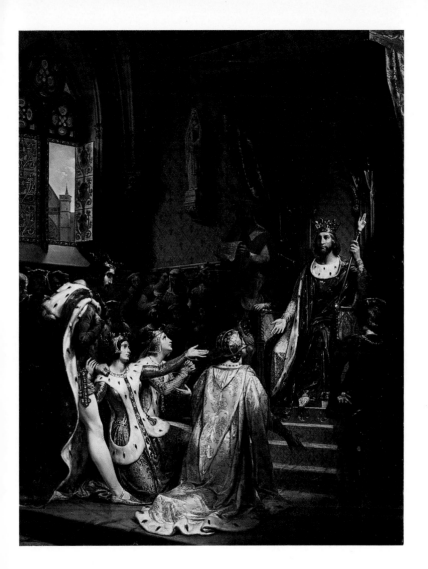

Merry Joseph BLONDEL. The King of Navarre Submits to Jean II in 1354 at the Louvre. *Musée National du Château de Versailles.*
Continuing to reside in the palace on the Ile de la Cité, the king only sat on the throne in the Louvre for very special occasions. Philippe le Bel convened a gathering of bishops and barons here in 1303 at the time of his disagreements with pope Boniface VIII. In 1313 he gave sumptuous feasts in honor of Edward, king of England, his son-in-law. The surrender of the King of Navarre is a diplomatic event that explains the choice of the Louvre for its symbolic value.

The artistic role of the Louvre began under Henri IV, who assembled a collection of Antiquities on the ground floor of the Petite Galerie. He also decided to provide artists' residences in the palace. Lodgings in the basement of the Grande Galerie were given to those artists who obtained official administrative approval.

More important was the entry of the Academies into the heart of the palace. The French Academy, already present since 1672, was joined by those of the Inscription and Belles Lettres. The Academy of Painting,

Gillot SAINT-EVRE. The Inauguration and Installation of the King's Library by Charles V in the Tour de la Librairie (Library Tower). *Musée National du Château de Versailles. Precious manuscripts from Charles V's collection are preserved on three richly paneled levels. Christine de Pisan affirms: "let us speak again of the wisdom of King Charles, the great love he had for study and knowledge, as for the most important books of holy scripture, theology, philosophy and all the sciences, many of which are well-written and richly adorned".*

Adolphe ROGER. The Dauphin Charles Entering the Louvre after Etienne Marcel's Assassination. *Musée National du Château de Versailles. The Louvre played an essential role in the political life of a troubled time. After the defeat at Poitiers, Jean le Bon was taken prisoner by the English. Etienne Marcel, provost of merchants, set himself up in opposition to a monarchy of little credibility and gave the people crossbows and lances that were held in reserve. After he in turn was killed in 1359, Charles V marked his victory over the lower-class uprising by a solemn march into the Louvre. It was at this time that he made the decision to have another wall built around Paris that would bear his name.*

ANONYMOUS. Altarpiece of the
Parliament of Paris (detail). *Musée du
Louvre, Paris.*
*As the backdrop of a familiar scene, the
Louvre appears here like a fairy castle.*

destined to play an important
role in the artistic life of the time,
took up residence on the first
floor, in rooms close to the
Galerie d'Apollon, that was
decorated by Charles Le Brun,
while the Academy of Antiques
settled in the caryatid room,
which was, at the time of the
Valois, the main reception hall.

The Royal Academy, whose
role in controlling artistic life was
all powerful, began organizing

Jean CLOUET. Portrait of François I.
Musée du Louvre, Paris.
*As a lover of paintings, François I invited
Italian painters to Fontainebleau, among
them Leonardo da Vinci, and so announced
his vocation as the sovereign collector. It was
from these royal acquisitions that the Louvre
Museum was born.* The Mona Lisa, *a key
work among them, entered the collection
through François I.*

exhibits of its members' work in the Cour Carrée in 1725, and originated the term 'salon' to describe the annual artistic events that determined the future and reputation of the artists who had the honor and good fortune to be admitted.

Versailles remained the center of power and administration for the monarchy until its fall in 1793. Left to its occupants, the Louvre lost some of its grandeur. It also suffered from the excessive parceling of its various wings,

and a profusion of parasitic constructions encroached on it. These buildings did not totally disappear until Napoléon III's projects rebuilding the area between the Tuileries and the Louvre, that lead to the Tuileries as the center of court life. Meanwhile, the Louvre (known as the old Louvre) remained a site for civil and artistic activities that were turbulent and disorganized, prompting Napoléon I to order Percier and Fontaine to intervene.

Anonymous. The Pont-Neuf and the Seine, circa 1633. *Musée National du Château de Versailles.*
Desired by Henri III, and completed under Henri IV, the Pont-Neuf reinforced the unity of the two banks of the Seine and prefigured modern Paris. The nearby Louvre found itself at the center of a city
that was growing up and arranging its public areas in symbolic order around it, as if it existed for that purpose. The urban landscape, with its restrained charm and discreet elegance, announced a society where the governing idea for urbanization and social bonds would be art and culture.

Though it had lost its grandeur and its original role, the Louvre had begun its career as a museum.

The idea of using the Louvre as a museum came from d'Angiviller, Marigny's successor at the post of General Director of the King's Buildings. It was simply a question of allowing the public to visit the collections that had been created by the various rulers. These collections already included 423 paintings, a number of which are still seen there today. It was actually a kind of warehouse for works that could be selected to decorate the various royal residences, but admitting the public introduced a change in mentalities and prefigured the museum that would emerge during the Revolution.

The Revolution interrupted the monarchy's projects but replaced them, often copying the original ideas, with others that would show a willingness to make art accessible to everyone. The

National Assembly included this idea in its program, after the events of August 10, 1793, and the Convention finally ratified the creation of the museum. This event was overseen by a commission directed by the painter David. The Louvre Museum was born.

The Louvre palace expanded together with the Tuileries palace, which provided it with an opulent facade facing the garden it gave its name to. Right up until its disappearance under the Commune (1871), the Tuileries palace not only polarized the social life of the monarchy, but also determined the various expansions of the Louvre itself. The ambition of each ruler was to link the two palaces, in order to give them the scale of their dreams of grandeur.

This process accelerated under Napoléon III, after his

ZEEMAN. View of the Old Louvre and the Petit Bourbon, from the Seine. *Musée du Louvre, Paris.*
The Pavillon du Roi, with the lengthening of the Renaissance wing and the Petite Galerie, constituted the greater part of the palace at that time, which had not yet freed itself from the remains of the medieval palace, a corner tower of which appears to the right. The activity along the Seine places the Louvre in the center of daily life.

predecessor had gotten rid of the artists who had been living in the Grande Galerie, and had confided the expansions on the rue de Rivoli side to Percier and Fontaine, and at the same time, developed the rigorous view of this street's undulating arcades.

Under Napoléon III, Visconti and Lefuel took charge of the new wings that greatly enlarged the old Louvre by framing it, and at the same time creating a series of inner courtyards, some of which can be seen in the tours offered by the museum today (the Marly, Puget, and Khorsabad courtyards on the rue de Rivoli side).

The Louvre now had its definitive form. The Tuileries Palace opened its western side and gave it a dynamic shape, creating continuity with the garden. The overall effect highlights the Arc de Triomphe

Henri TESTELIN. Colbert Presenting the Members of the Royal Academy of Science to Louis XIV in 1667. Musée National du Château de Versailles. The Academy of Science was housed in the royal apartments (ground floor) and held its meetings in the Salle Henri II. Their equipment was placed in the Salle des Gardes (today La Caze).

Jean-Baptiste ISABEY. The Stairway of the Napoleon Museum. Musée du Louvre, Paris.

According to Victor Baltard, "the arrangement adopted for the Napoleon Museum required that a new stairway be built to serve both as a flight of steps and to connect with the painting galleries. The location of the Grand Salon, the Galerie d'Apollon and painting galleries determined that it be placed to the right of the entrance vestibule. That is why we thought it best to build it where the Salle de Comédie, built by Henri IV, used to be, near the queen's apartments. This staircase should have two entrances, be a double spiral and have twenty-two marble columns". In 1855, the entrance to the museum was moved and the staircase partially destroyed to make way for the Daru staircase that is now there, leading to the Winged Victory of Samothrace. *On the other hand, the Percier and Fontaine rooms are still there with their sumptuous decor, ceilings decorated by Charles Meunier (*France under the Shafts of Minerva Protecting the Arts*) and Nicolas Gosse's medallions.*
At the top of the staircase is the Salle Duchatel, preceding the Salon Carré and the Grande Galerie. The ceiling is decorated with The Triumph of French Painting *,* Apotheosis of Poussin, Le Sueur and Le Brun *by Charles Meynier.*

Auguste COUDER. Percier and Fontaine
Showing Napoleon the Plans for a
Staircase in the Museum. *Musée du
Louvre, Paris.*
*To provide an appropriate setting for the
artistic treasures he gathered along his path
of glory, Napoleon entrusted Percier and
Fontaine with a radical restructuring of the
Louvre. The interior of the Pavillon du Roi
and the southern wing of the Cour Carrée
were dramatically altered. Stone vaults,*
*sumptuous galleries decorated with red
marble and a new entrance with its set of
staircases designed to make the best use of
the space, gave it a certain grandeur which
bespoke the spirit of the museum; a place of
glory, and a display of riches. Napoleon's
megalomania is extended to glorifying art
in the spirit of Roman emperors and, like
them, he would parade works of art
through the streets before setting them into
the pompous decor created for them.*

Victor Joseph CHAVET. The Louvre of Napoleon III. *Musée National du Château, Compiègne.*
With its surroundings finally cleared and its connection to the Tuileries palace accomplished, the Louvre palace found its definitive form. Credit is due to Napoleon III, the principal contractor, who is celebrated by a medallion that shows the emperor-builder's satisfaction.

du Carrousel, as well as today's pyramid. These final touches added to a general concept of the palace that has come through time without ever losing the miraculous unity and harmony that set off the different styles, linking their diverse qualities. They bear witness, charmingly, to the entire history of the French monarchy (from the Capetians on), and, by being the most complete monument in France, this is a kind of anthology of its history.

Joseph *Auguste*. The Crown Jewels Room. *Musée du Louvre, Paris.*
In the beginning, the Louvre Museum obeyed the principles of presentation which was forced to play upon the *existing decor of the palace and at the same time display the taste for splendor that accompanies art. A room of the museum was more like a sumptuous sitting room, heavy with ornamentation.*

Palace Decoration

*T*hough nothing of the
decorations of the original
Louvre remains (apart from a
few scraps presented in the room
devoted to the history of the
Louvre), some of the elements
that comprised the king's
residence are still there to be
seen. The museum has not
entirely covered the wealth of the
monarchy nor the different
decorative touches added by
successive reigns, nor the dreams
of grandeur that followed.

François I was the first who
wanted to replace the medieval
structure with architecture in a
Renaissance spirit. He called
upon Pierre Lescot, who was
helped by Jean Goujon, which
explains the many sculptures
finely presented on the two
corner wings that close off the
Cour Carrée at the west and
south. As a kind of primer for
the future palace, they were
treated with exquisite grace and
decorated with an
overabundance of divinity,
renowned personages, trophies,
and allegories sculpted by
Etienne Cramoy, Pierre Manyn,
Lefort, and the Lheureux
brothers who worked alongside
Jean Goujon.

Colonnade.

When Colbert took on the completion of the Louvre for the glory of Louis XIV, he organized a competition for the eastern façade and several projects were proposed. Among these was one by Bernini that used curves and counter-curves in a lyrical flight that was contradictory to the overall spirit of the building. The design selected was the one generally attributed to Claude Perrault (the brother of Charles, famous for his fairy tales). He was an anatomist by training with a rigorous spirit who considered architecture to be an extension of the laws that govern the human body. He perfected and supervised a highly developed, well-lit work of magnificent order, which was in fact the revival of an earlier project by Léonor Houdin, reworked by Mansart and d'Orbay. In the end, it was a collective achievement.

From 1546 to 1574 (up until the reign of Henri III) the king's residence was enlarged by the successive construction of the buildings south of what is now the Cour Carrée, work that was begun by Lescot and completed by Androuet du Cerceau. The main entrance of the palace was the central avant-corps that opens directly onto the Salle des Suisses (the Caryatid Room), then used for celebrations. It can still be seen, with its rostrum beneath Jean Goujon's caryatids,

The ceiling of Louis XIV's bedchamber.

The ceiling that decorated Louis XIV's bedchamber in the Pavillon du Roi (which is now the Salle des Sept Cheminées) was removed and placed in the Colonnade wing by a team directed by Gilles Guérin. The cabinet maker Louis Barrois had made it in 1654. The central painting, attributed to Le Sueur, has disappeared, but there remain figures by François Girardon, Thomas Regnaudin, Nicolas Legendre and Laurent Magnier.

inspired by the story of Erechtheus. Though the rostrum has lost its original balustrade, it was embellished during the First Empire with Benvenuto Cellini's Diane of Anet (today, a copy is seen there). The current ceiling, the work of Lemercier, dates back to the time of Louis XIII, and replaced the original beamed ceiling. Percier and Fontaine later added to its decoration. A portico, framed with columns, separates it from the old tribunal hall that led to the king's pavilion.

The royal residence was dramatically altered during the reign of Charles X, while the museum was being established. He had Fontaine bring back some of the decorative elements, adding them to the new adjacent rooms, and these are a fine example of the luxury that the king reveled in while living in the Louvre.

Henri II's parade room has a ceiling and door leaves sculpted by Scibec de Carpi, whose work had already been seen at the Fontainebleau Chateau. The Louis XIV room is decorated with a ceiling by Gilles Guerin, and Girardon and Regnauldin helped with its decorative sculptures.

When the Charles X museum was set up in what had been the royal apartments, the layout was built around a series of rooms whose ceilings were painted by the official artists of the time. The manifesto-painting was done by Ingres, and it shows Homer triumphant in front of an antique temple, with the Iliad and the Odyssey depicted as figures

laying dreamily at his feet. The seduction of Greco-Roman culture, that all of the official painters freely copied, is clearly apparent here. From ceiling to ceiling, one can follow the wrath of the poet inspired by a sort of grace and soppy elegance that reduces its strength, civilizing it

Caryatid Room (Salle des Cariatides). *This was the room for pomp and ceremony at the Louvre during the Valois dynasty. At that time it was the heart of the palace, the spectacle for court life that was at the same time sumptuous and gallant, roguish and cruel, cynical and torn by the religious conflicts that would culminate in the Saint Bartholomew Day massacre.*

according to the canons of the time.

The Salle des Sept Cheminées was built in the location of the king's apartments, on the first floor of the Pavillon du Roi. One is particularly drawn to the ornamentation of the monumental ceiling, which is extremely high, having taken some of its space from the attic. Its decorative richness in no way detracts from its moldings. The museographic role of the room is clearly signified by a series of medallion portraits in hexagonal recesses that run along a festooned decor: we see Guerin, Gerard, Gros, David, Girodet, Granet, Géricault, Chaudet, Proudhon and Percier - an implicit acknowledgment of the artists recognized at that time (1850). Here an overall organization is accentuated in the corners by composite trophies

Léon COGNIET. Ceiling of the Salle Campana: The Egyptian Expedition. *A suite of rooms, parallel with those of the Charles X Museum, was installed in the space created by Le Vau in order to double the southern wing of the Cour Carrée in 1668. The collection by Revoil, a 'troubador' artist, was placed there in 1828, and the decoration was entrusted to the painters and sculptors in fashion at* that time. *The general theme chosen was the history of France. The ceiling of the first room is the work of Léon Cogniet entitled,* The Egyptian Expedition under the Orders of Bonaparte. *It is accompanied by arches with bas-reliefs showing consecutively* The Battle of Aboukir, The Revolt of Cairo, The Cairo Revolt being Pardoned, *and* The Plague of Jaffa.

initialed RF (République Française), a sign of the museum's belonging to a generous new Republic that saw this as an expression of its cultural dynamism.

Going under the caryatid tribune, one reaches the Grand Degré, the flight of stairs that dates back to the time of Henry II. It was one of the entrances of the

Staircase of Honor, ground floor.
The progressive move from a residence to a museum necessitated an interior architecture that constantly shifted between two contradictory functions. The museum is also, in a certain way, a luxurious house.

palace, and its arch was made by Jean Goujon and his assistants. The Grand Degré leads to the first floor and the former royal apartments. The many transformations of the palace make it very difficult to locate the original rooms. All that remains of the royal decor are scraps ripped from the walls and ceilings that were removed to create the Salle des Sept Cheminées. This room, which is basically the same size as it was then, was the central seat of power from Henri II to Louis XIV.

The familiar decor of the kings, moved to the Colonnade suite, is a good indication of the luxury they surrounded themselves with to ensure their credibility and the proper observance of the rites necessitated by contact with the people. These rites remained voluntarily flexible, as long as they were accompanied by the marks of respect required by hierarchy.

The south wing, built by Pierre Lescot, was doubled in size by Louis Le Vau and became a museum under Napoléon I. His architects, Percier and Fontaine, undertook renovations of the Queen's former apartments, which had, in the interim, been occupied by the Royal Academy. It was under Charles X that a general decorative theme was established. This included nine rooms, richly decorated by Ingres, François Joseph Heim, Charles Meynier, Edouard Picot, Abel de Pujol, Horace Vernet and Baron Gros. At the same time, in the space created by Louis le Vau when he expanded this southern wing, the Campana Gallery was extended, and it too was decorated by artists selected by Hector Lefuel. There were, respectively, works by Léon Cogniet, Dröelling, Victor Schnetz, Alexandre Evariste Fragonard, François-Joseph Heim, Devéria and Jean Allaux. This is a typical example of the period's artistic ideals, marked by a taste for Orientalism and the style of the Troubadours.

Just like the first floor, the ground floor of the oldest part of the Louvre, which had contained the Queen's apartments, was heavily renovated to give the space the sober elegance required for exhibiting ancient works. Fontaine radically altered the original divisions to obtain an open space that ran parallel to Le Vau's extensions along the Seine and the Jardin de l'Infante - a two-tone marble decor in red and gray, which alternated with arches. This combination gives excellent views all the way to the adjoining wing on the east side, under the Colonnade of the Galerie Henri IV. Nothing at all remains of the palace that lodged kings, and its museographic function has created its own style of grandeur and solemnity.

The passage leading to the Petite Galerie from the Pavillon du Roi was also enlarged during the large renovations undertaken by Le Vau in 1660. The king's antechamber and wardrobe were combined to form a vast receiving room. This room served as a connecting room, and its ceiling was originally decorated by Merry-Joseph Blondel, but was later taken down, replaced by the sometimes contested

Giovanni Francesco ROMANELLI.
The drawing room of the queen
mother, Anne of Austria's summer
apartment: Spring.
*The antechamber was baptized, the Salle
des Saisons. It was decorated by Anguier*
and Romanelli who painted Apollo and
the Muses, Diana and Acteon, Apollo
and Marsyas *and* Diane and
Endymion *on the ceiling and the*
Seasons *at the corners.*

painting by Georges Braque, whose simple birds fly around the original delicate wooden decor of Francisque Scibec de Carpi, who had already painted the ceiling of the royal bedchamber.

When it was originally built, the Lemercier wing at the north of the Cour Carrée served only to close off the space and provide aesthetic coherence. At one time, it contained trysting rooms for courtesans. In 1825, Percier and Fontaine were asked to create a suite of rooms for the Conseil d'Etat. The decoration for this was done by painters in favor at the time: Merry-Joseph Blondel, Drölling and Jean-Baptiste Mauzaisse. The Salon de Beauvais (taking its name from the street that ran close by before the Rue de Rivoli was built) was included in the continuity of the state council rooms. The ceiling was decorated with an important work by Carolus-Duran.

Framed by two imposing staircases, the Colonnade wing, originally designed to contain the king's lodgings, remained unfinished for a long time. To the north, the sculptural decoration (the Assyrian staircase) was commissioned from four artists; Jacques-Edme Dumont, Barthélemy-François Chardigny, Antoine Moutony and Pierre-Charles Bridan. To the south, where Jacques-Louis David had his workshop, and where he painted the *The Intervention of the Sabine Women*, Percier and Fontaine built the Egyptian staircase, also called the Midi

staircase. Four other sculptors, François-Antoine Gérard, Auguste Taunay, Félix Fortin and Charles-Antoine Callamard, were responsible for its decoration.

The Cour Carrée

Problems of unification arose when the Louvre was completed, the Renaissance wing extended and original courtyard quadrupled in size. Building on the work of Pierre Lescot, that had been continued by Lemercier, Le Vau had to consider these buildings to ensure the right angles of the buildings he was raising. Having commissioned the Colonnade from Perrault, he was responsible for designing the interior.

To maintain continuity, Lemercier commissioned the sculptural decoration of the Pavillon de l'Horloge from Gilles Guerin, Philippe de Buyster and Thibaud Poissant, who took inspiration from the drawings of Jacques Sarrazin. This wing, that matched the one built by Pierre Lescot, was only decorated much later by Jean-Guillaume Moitte, Philippe Rolad and Antoine Chaudet.

The Louis Le Vau wings also contain sculptures used as decorations. It was Jacques-Ange Gabriel who started re-doing the eastern facade while Coustou created the pediment. Finally, under Napoléon I, Percier and Fontaine completed the task of unification and had Lesueur and Claude Ramey handle its sculptural ornamentation.

Anne of Austria's apartment.
*All that remains of Anne of Austria's
apartment is the ceiling. Her series of
rooms were taken out to create one long
room broken up by framed porticoes and
antique columns.*

The Petite Galerie

The construction of the Tuileries Palace, by Catherine de Medicis, quickly inspired the idea of connecting it to the kings' palace, but the two buildings were some distance apart, divided by the Charles V wall and the development of a heavily-populated quarter around the Louvre itself.

The Petite Galerie was the beginning of a project that would assume all the magnitude of the original plan imagined along with the Grand Galerie that it set off from the Louvre, placing it parallel to the Seine. A short passage linking the Pavillon du

Giovanni Francesco ROMANELLI. The ceiling of the Salle des Sévères: Esther and Assuerus; Hercules français.
This room was formerly two rooms, the queen's bedchamber and study. For the bedchamber, Romanelli designed various mythological scenes as well as scenes inspired by the Bible (among them, Esther and Assuerus). Reunited as one room under the Consulate, the false ceiling of the study was taken out revealing the decoration made by Hennequin who produced a French depiction of Hercules.

Roi with the Petite Galerie was built over the moat of the old Louvre. Its ground floor long served as a simple passageway, but under Anne of Austria, it became the Queen's apartment. It is a series of rooms starting with the Rotonde de Mars, followed by the Salle de Mécène room, the queen's antechamber (the Salle des Saisons), the vestibule (the Salon de la Paix, that led to the Jardin de l'Infante to the east and to a courtyard to the west, now called the Cour du Sphinx), the queen's study (the Salle Severe), the bedchamber, and the small study (the Salle des Antonins). Le Vau took charge of the decor for this imposing apartment, and some of the ceilings painted by Romanelli and some of the stucco work by Michel Auguier remain, although under the Consulat there were major transformations - the ceilings in the Salle de Mécène were redone by Meynier, and those in the Salle des Antonins by Hennequin - as it was to become a museum of antiquities at that time. It was inaugurated on November 7, 1800 by Napoléon Bonaparte. The

The Galerie d'Apollon.
The first floor, a portrait gallery of monarchs, was destroyed by fire in 1661. The only portrait that survived from this collection is the Marie de Médicis *by Pourbus. Le Vau created a sumptuous decor to the glory of the Sun King. It was a kind of dress rehearsal before undertaking the Château de Versailles, where the decorative arrangements combined painting, plasters and sculpture. Le Brun focused on mural painting around the plaster work of* François Girardon, the Gaspard brothers, Balthasard Marsy, and Thomas Regnaudin. As the seat of the Royal Academy of Painting, whatever was left unpainted was then painted by its members (Jean-Hugues Taraval, Jean Jacques Lagrenée, François Callet, Renou). During the final stages of restoration by Duban, Joseph Guichard and Charles-Louis Muller were called in. The work done by Delacroix constitutes the most remarkable section of the overall work.

View of the room with the Venus de Milo.
This was formerly the queens' apartments. The queen mother inhabited the ground floor when the reigning queen was in residence on the first floor. Catherine de Médicis was succeeded by Anne of Austria here. The architect Fontaine took out the apartments for the museum and antiquities were placed here. There is a magnificent view of the Venus de Milo.

The staircase leading to the Winged Victory of Samothrace.
The first entrance to the museum was via the Napoleon staircase. During the museum's expansion, Lefuel built a monumental staircase for the Pavillon Daru lit by cupolas that also served the Old Louvre and the wing parallel to the Grande Galerie. The staircase remained incomplete due to the fall of the Second Empire but work was taken up again by Edmond Guillaume in 1883. To give it

arrangement of the rooms responded to a desire to highlight the two most important works: *The Laocoon* (in the Salle des Antonins) and the *Apollo Belvedere* (in the Salle d'Auguste). The museum was entered through the Sphinx courtyard.

The outside sculpted decor completed the original ornamentation by Barthelemy Prieur.

The Galerie d'Apollon

It was under Henri IV that the first floor of the Petite Galerie was decorated, by Bunel and Flament, with portraits of the kings and queens of France from Saint-Louis onwards, and its ceiling depicted scenes taken from the old testament. Destroyed by a fire in 1661, it was restored by Le Vau, and Charles Le Brun was responsible for the work. He exalted the Sun King, hence the reference to Apollo, which he did not have time to finish painting.

The Academy of Painting used this room until 1793, adding to the decor with works by Renou, Lagrenée le Jeune, Durameau and Taraval.

greater majesty, the Winged Victory of Samothrace, *found on the island of Samothrace in 1863 (hence its name), was placed at the top of the staircase, gloriously crowning its flight. The precision of its proportions and the sober grandeur of the sculpture offer exceptional and exemplary beauty in which the fundamental concepts of the museum are incarnated: a place for exalting form and thought, a repository for civilization and transcendent mankind.*

The works begun by Duban in 1848, in response to needs for security, allowed Delacroix to put the final touches to it with *Apollo Conquering a Python* which justified the name of the gallery. It then became the showcase for the crown jewels.

The Grande Galerie

This is the Pavillon des Ambassadeurs, built by Louis Metezeau, that links the Petite Galerie (built under Catherine de Medicis by Pierre Lescot) with the Grande Galerie. The Salon Carré was created there, during modifications made by Le Vau.

The basements of the Grande Galerie date from 1566 but were completed under Henri IV in 1607. A section by Louis Métézeau (up to the Pavillon de Lesdiguieres) continues right up to the Pavillon de Flore, built by Jacques Androuet du Cerceau. This was considerably altered by Duban during the Second Republic, then completed by Lefuel, at the same time as the Pavillon de Flore that closed it off to the west, and that created the connection with the old Tuileries Palace.

To preserve the building from being degraded by passersby, and from vandalism that had damaged the previous construction so much, it was isolated by a longitudinal moat, in the English style, which also gave light to its lower rooms.

In its first section, the Grande Galerie was cut through by an overhanging door (called the Barbet de Jouy door). This was the former entrance from the river. A large balcony built over this door was decorated majestically by Duban.

At the site of the former Saint-Nicaise gate, that had been enlarged by Marigny in 1759 by a triple arcade, Duban designed the Carrousel entrance gate, set in between the Lesdiguieres and Tremoille pavilions, and decorated with two monumental sculptures by Jouffroy dedicated to the *Merchant Marine* and the *Navy*, which dominated a sculpture of *Apollo Riding Pegasus* by Mercié. Between this sculpture and the Pavillon de Flore, Lefuel placed a door called the Emperor, or Lion door, because of the animal sculptures that framed it. Several of the pediments that provided continuity in the development of the gallery were the work of Crauk, Perrey and especially Carrier-Belleuse.

The Grande Galerie, which was a connecting gallery that facilitated a discreet escape from the old Louvre, was designated as a residence for artists and craftsmen working for the crown, or in favor with the king.

Among the many occupants of this singular phalanstery were: Fragonard, who sketched pleasant scenes of his family life; Pigalle, the sculptor; the Sylvestre dynasty; the painter Regnault; the pastellist La Tour; Isabey; the future general director of the museum, Vivant-Denon, who was then a brilliant young aristocrat and author of a libertine novel; Pajou; Greuze, the cuckold; Lagrenée; Carle

The Napoleon III apartment, the Grand Salon.

The conversion of the apartments for the Ministry of State residing in the Richelieu wing was entrusted to Lefuel. He chose ostentatious, extravagant luxury. The rooms were deliberately adjoining to provide space for the receptions so often held there and a theater salon was even *included to enliven the evenings. Louis Alphonse Tranchant established the model for abundance with as much gilt as stucco and as many draperies as trimmings. The ceiling pays homage to the imperial couple. Napoleon III held a celebration to honor the linking of the Louvre with the Tuileries palaces, which was the dream of monarchs from the palaces' origins.*

Vernet who succeeded the cabinetmaker Boulle; and last but not least, Hubert Robert, thanks to whom we have an astonishing account of the Grande Galerie in his sketches and fantastical images of ruins.

His contribution is a major chapter in the history of the museum, as he addressed the problems of presentation, lighting and use of space that had not been designed for this role, and how a palace becomes a museum without giving up the decoration that is its own.

It was in the Salon Carré, at the end of the Grande Galerie, that the exhibits of the Academicians were held from 1725. These exhibits gave birth to the term 'Salon', and booklets were published for each of them. After having originally taken place every year, they then took place every two years. They were the most important events of the artistic year. In 1848, the architect Duban set the Salon Carré up as an exhibit room where the most famous paintings were presented. It was, in a sense, the heart of the museum at that time. The ceiling also had to conform with the contents of the room and complement its moldings. The responsibility for evoking the different arts allegorically - painting, engraving, sculpture - was given to the sculptor Simard. His works are both strong and pensive, evoking, respectively, Pierre Lescot, Jean Goujon, Nicolas Poussin, and Jean Pesne. In 1972 a final adaptation, to its current role, was made.

The Grande Galerie of Hubert Robert

Living in the Louvre and responsible, by a decree signed by d'Angiviller, for the "custody" of the museum, Hubert Robert greatly contributed to its creation. His mission (with the help of a commission) was to think about how the former king's residence could be adapted to exhibit works of art. The paintings of the royal collections were scattered about the various residences of the crown, the superintendancy of Buildings of Versailles (1122 pieces), and the Luxembourg Gallery (116 pieces), from where the important series *The Life of Marie de Médicis* by Rubens came in 1785, as well as the Louvre, which had its own storeroom. A vast purchasing campaign then began, and Hubert Robert acted as curator. The fall of the monarchy upset this institution, but the "Assemblée Constituante" reconstituted it in 1792. The museum opened on August 10, 1793, but without Hubert Robert, who did not return to his post until 1795, along with Fragonard, Pajou and Wailly.

The Grande Galerie had been filled with relief maps of the cities and fortresses of France since 1697. To meet its new role, it needed to be refurbished, and this task was entrusted successively to Soufflot, de Wailly, and Clérisseau. Hubert Robert was part of the commission of 1778 responsible for studying the feasibility of these projects.

Though he only had a secondary and occasional role in defining the museum, it so intimately reflects his own Ruinistic vision that he is forever associated with it. The series of paintings that he selected for the Grande Galerie are in fact a precious chronicle of his life as a remarkable creator of what would become museography, and the art of transforming a royal palace into a museum, without altering its spirit too much. He was at the heart of a problem that has remained present and that has dominated all the projects that have progressively transformed the Louvre palace into the largest museum in the world.

Hubert ROBERT. Project for Decoration of the Grande Galerie. *Musée du Louvre, Paris.*
Though he exaggerated the length for theatrical effect, Hubert Robert offered a veritable architectural program for the Grande Galerie which included the segmentation of the gallery to achieve greater visibility of the collections as well as better use of overhead light. Copyists are seen who, at that time, 'had their day' and abounded as the Louvre served as a pedagogical function before becoming an instrument of pure delight.

The subject of this reflective exercise was the Grande Galerie, since this was the heart of the future museum. It also played a role, because of its own configuration and poetry, in the themes developed in Piranese's entourage, and Hubert Robert was an excellent continuator. He was more pragmatic than his master, but brought to practical problems the poetic force that had been promulgated by the spirit of the Ruinists at the end of the 18th century.

We owe the division of the long hall into nine bays to Percier and Fontaine, while Lefuel proceeded to install the overhead lighting that Hubert Robert had already imagined.

Abandoned by Louis XIV when he moved to Versailles, the Louvre suffered a long period of decadence accelerated by the arrival of various uncertain and authoritative institutions and artists who lived there together in a noisy and nonchalant manner, obviously compromising the proper upkeep of the place.

Having taken up residence in the Tuileries, the Revolutionaries left the Louvre as it was, imagining that they would put their "museum" in the Grande Galerie, and working only toward this goal, they merely readapted a project that had already been drawn up during the reign of Louis XVI.

It was Napoléon I, in his vast program of urbanization and renewal of official sites, in conformity with his reign, and in the spirit and style that he promoted, who ordered improvements to accommodate works of art that would be taken from every country he conquered in the form of war booty. Residing in the Tuileries palace, it was there that he would leave his mark. Extending the improvement program of the Grande Galerie begun by the Revolution, he decided to put the museum of antiquities in the apartments of Anne of Austria, going ahead with modifications that hinted at a Louvre much more open to the public.

The Restoration did little other than comfort the Louvre in its new role as museum, with Charles X overseeing the vast transfer of decorations from the old royal apartments to the Colonnade wing. The museum grew to the detriment of its original environment.

Napoléon III completed the long-awaited unification of the Louvre and Tuileries palaces, and gave the new wings on the Rivoli side to certain of his administrative services. Among these were the apartments that were to be occupied for a very long time by the Finance Ministry. It contained such incredibly rich decoration of such extraordinary, sometimes excessive wealth, that it was an anthology of the style of the Second Empire. Velvet-covered benches, baskets of flowers, a greenhouse atmosphere and all the ostentatious luxury of a society of *nouveau riches* with voluptuous mores. This was more of a private dwelling than an official palace wielding power. The symbols for this power were missing. The Louvre was no longer the palace of kings but of the luxury of a nation that delighted in its riches. Merchants and bankers replaced knights and the nobility of the court. This was an opulent reign, no longer hiding its vices, sliding toward ostentation, where affluence mingled with power.

The completion of the Louvre under Napoléon III followed a logic that meant to correct the absence of parallelism between the north and south wings and break the monotony of development of the building that had been uniform for too long. What resulted are the high pavilions: Turgot, Richelieu and Colbert to the north, and Mollien, Denon and Daru to the south. These all recall the Pavillon de l'Horloge of Lemercier, but with an abundance of decoration, typical of the period, an overload which included sculptures by Georges Diebolt (Pavillon de Rohan), Pierre Cavelier and Eugène Guillaume (Pavillon Turgot), Francisque Duret, Bosio and Barye (Pavillon Richelieu), Victor Vilain (Pavillon Colbert), Barye, Simart and Duret (Pavillon Sully), Simart - a *Napoléon Surrounded by Peace and the Arts*,

Hubert ROBERT. Project for Decoration of the Grande Galerie. *Musée du Louvre, Paris.*
The Grande Galerie is represented just as it was before its transformation by Percier and Fontaine in 1805. The presentation of paintings crammed into picture rails was a *practice that endured until the 20th century. Even though he painted only part of the gallery (here looking toward the Pavillon de Flore), Hubert Robert, by an artistic method, exaggerated the perspective which fades into an effect of mist, lengthening the space more than it was in reality.*

which is the only effigy of the sovereign in Paris - Barye's groups (Pavillon Denon), and François Jouffroy and Eugene Lequesne (Pavillon Mollien).

Added to this was a veritable gallery of French cultural celebrities decorating the interior of the Cour Napoleon. The passage running from the Pavillon du Rohan to the Pavillon Lesdiguieres included busts and sculptures of La Fontaine, Pascal, Molière, Boileau, Fénelon, La Rochefoucauld, Corneille, Grégoire de Tours, Rabelais, Malherbe, Abélard, Colbert, Mazarin, Buffon, Froissard, J.J.Rousseau, Montesquieu, Turgot, La Bruyère, Suger,

Hubert ROBERT. Project for Decoration of the Grande Galerie. Musée du Louvre, Paris.
Hubert Robert shows the Grande Galerie in its state prior to the intervention of Percier and Fontaine. The concept of the museum was the same as that of the collector's studio, with an accumulation of works in picture rails.

Bourdaloue, Racine, Voltaire, Bossuet, Condorcet, Papin, Sully, Vauban, Lavoisier, Louvois, Saint-Simon, Joinville, Commynes, Mignard, Massillon, du Cerceau, Claude Lorrain, Grétry, Regnard, Jacques Coeur, Chenier, Jean Goujon, Coysevox, Jean Cousin, Le Nôtre, Clodion, Germain Pilon, Lemercier, Descartes, Ambroise Pare, Richelieu, Montaigne, Houdon, Coustou, Le Sueur, Perrault, Philippe de

Champaigne, Puget, Pierre Lescot, Bullant, Le Brun, Philibert Delorme and Bernard Palissy.

During its reconstruction by Lefuel, the Pavillon de Flore was crowned with a vast composition by Jean-Baptiste Carpeaux, and framed by the works of Pierre Cavelier and Jules Franceschi. Three sides of the Pavillon de Marsan were decorated with works by Gustave Crauk, Jean-Marie Bonassieux and Théodore Gruyère.

View from the room with the Stanga palace door and Michelangelo's Slaves.
The Michelangelo Gallery was formerly the Galerie Mollien. It is accessible, like the Salle Daru opposite it, through the Denon wing. This was the main entrance to the museum up until the final stages of the Grand Louvre project. The design of these two galleries was inspired by the Caryatid Room. The view is softened by the ceiling vaults and the different geometrically shaped marble tiles.

Major events at the Louvre

In a political climate of escalating power which pitted him against Henri V and Charles Quint, François I used architecture to assert his supremacy. The idea of transforming the old fortress into a prestigious residence was born of his desire to win admiration and assert power. In 1539-1540, sumptuous parties were held in the palace under construction in honor of Charles-Quint's visit with François I. "The castle was made so livable," recounts Sauval, "that Charles-Quint, the king, the queen, the Dauphin, the Dauphine, the king's brothers and sisters along with the other children of royal lineage, the king and queen of Navarre, the Cardinal of Tournon, the supreme commander of the French army and the Duchess of Étampes and the mistress of François I were all lodged in apartments equal to their station. So many expenditures were made that they filled an entire royal register." According to the historian André Blum: "the courtyard was transformed, the weather vanes gilded, the old Charles V buildings hidden behind

A palace of kings, a seat of power, a city of the fortunate, their families and the festivities that punctuate the life of the court, the Louvre has been the setting for all kinds of events.

Though François I initiated its construction, he died just before the work was finished. The Court of the Valois then used the Louvre to display its wealth and drama in a feverish climate of luxury and debauchery, intrigue and passion that culminated with the Saint Bartholomew day massacre.

In 1558, the princely marriages of Claude de France with the Duc de Lorraine, and that of the dauphin François (future François II) with Marie Stuart, were celebrated in the salle des fêtes (the Salle des Cariatides), as were the engagements, in 1559, of Elizabeth de France with Philippe II, King of Spain, and of the Princess Marguerite, sister of Henri IV with the Duke Philibert-Emmanuel de Savoie.

It was also here, on August 18, 1572, that the marriage of Henri de Bourbon, King of Navarre, the future Henri IV, was celebrated with Marguerite de Valois, the mad Queen Margot, and sister of Charles IX. Sumptuous feasts were given together with ballets and plays, in a carnival atmosphere. On August 22, Admiral Coligny was shot, and this marked the beginning of the horrible massacres between Catholics and modern decor and windows ornamented with pillars and painted moldings. The emperor's and the king's and queen's arms could be seen everywhere. According to an Italian account of Charles-Quint's voyage, a gigantic golden statue of Vulcan holding a lit flame was erected in the courtyard.

All the rooms were hung with tapestries of silk, gold and silver thread. There were performances, ballets, tournaments, and lance competitions, but all this luxury was discordant with the medieval architecture of the castle."

Protestants. "Blood and death were so rife in the streets that their majesties themselves, who had ordered the massacre, could only hide in fear in the Louvre," reported a witness.

Henri III (1575) organized masquerades, banquets and balls at the Louvre, and these were famous throughout Europe. The most famous of these was given for the marriage of his "mignon", the Duc de Joyeuse, to Marguerite de Lorraine, his own wife's sister.

Carried away by excess, enraging the people of Paris, this doleful and lavish king escaped from the Louvre on the day of the Barricades, helped by his cousin, Guise (May 12, 1588). He would never return.

The reign of Henri IV took shape in a climate of greater dignity. In 1593, the Duc de Mayenne presided over the Etats

ANONYMOUS, *French School 15th century.*
A Ball Held on September 24, 1581 at the Court of Henri III for the Wedding of Anne Duke de Joyeuse and Marguerite de Lorraine. *Musée du Louvre, Paris.*
The Salle des Cariatides and that of the first floor (today the Salle La Caze) were the setting of numerous celebrations held by a refined and gallant court. Ronsard praised it; Brantome observed it. Rare paintings recreate the outrageous character of these celebration, like a masquerade party, where people readily donned masks.

Alexandre Évariste FRAGONARD. Scene from the Saint Bartholomew Day Massacre in the Apartment of the Queen of Navarre. *Musée du Louvre, Paris.*
The darkest and bloodiest page in the history of the Louvre was the night of the

48

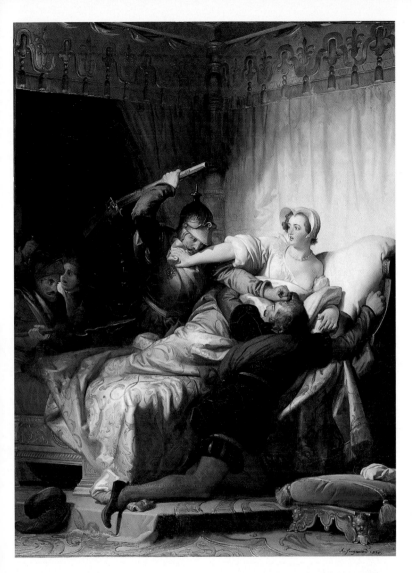

feast of Saint Bartholomew. The massacre
of Protestants encouraged by Charles IX,
in which legend has it that he
participated personally, was pursued
right into the antechambers and alcoves
of the palace. A ferocity that marks a
strange counterpoint to the refined
decadence and celebrations held in the
same place by the same people. These
tragic events, where the Louvre acted as a
stage, have often inspired painters of
history. The Son of the "good Frago" was
no exception, playing upon the style of
Romantic theater.

Généraux in the Salle Haute (the Salle La Caze) to put an end to the conflicts brought about by the wars of religion, and opened the Louvre to the new king. He made life here happier, together with his family.

This did not preclude celebrations for those at court whose births, marriages or deaths became national events, such as the marriage of César de Vendôme, the legitimate son of Henri IV and Gabrielle d'Estrées, with Françoise de Lorraine, daughter of the Duc de Mercoeur. Death was also celebrated, like the ceremonies that accompanied the exposition of Henri IV's effigy from the June 10 to 21, 1610. While the body was placed in a leaded coffin in

Adam Frans VAN DE MEULEN. Audience between Representatives of the Thirteen Swiss Cantons and King Louis XIV, in the Louvre. *Musée National du Château de Versailles.*
The arrival of ambassadors was the occasion for sumptuous ceremonies. The French Guard and the Archers were grouped under the entrance to the Louvre, the Swiss Guard on the steps of the Henri II staircase and the bodyguards in the Grande Salle. From here the ambassador was led to the parade room of the king. Louis XIV was more inclined to give his audiences in the Grand Cabinet or the Salon du Dôme.

the Salle de Parade (on the first floor), the crowd filed past a stage raised across from the main entrance on the ground floor, where a mannequin, with a wax head representing the king, lay in state. It was dressed in a red satin doublet and a purple velvet robe, decorated with fleur-de-lis and lined with ermine, and held a scepter and the hand of justice,

Jean ALAUX. The Etats Généraux
Gathered in the Salle de Bourbon of
the Louvre by Louis XIII. *Musée
National du Château de Versailles.*
*The discomfort and cramped space in the
rooms of the Louvre hindered large
gatherings, so it became habitual to
organize them in the Grande Salle de
Bourbon which was thirty-six meters
long by sixteen meters wide. At one end
there was a semi-circle fourteen meters
by seventeen and a beautiful vault
decorated with golden fleur-de-lis. This
room was superb when lit by its 1,200
white wax candles placed on consoles
and silver candleholders.*

the symbols of royal power. One
hundred masses were said over
an altar that had been built there
for the occasion, and, on the day
of the burial, the young Louis XIII,
9 years old and dressed in purple,
entered the room through the
tribunal to salute his late father
who was then taken for burial in
Saint-Denis. Such gestures
defined the protocol guiding

the life of the court through the medium of the most powerful symbol that it possessed.

Alternating between merry-making and romantic intrigues, and crimes the state justified for reasons of its own, life at the Louvre continued with bloody moments like the assassination of Concini, the Marquis d'Ancre, husband of Leonora Caligai, and childhood friend of Marie de Medicis on April 24, 1617. This event offended the young king, but other, more agreeable, events, such as the presentation of Corneille's *Nicomède* and Molière's *The Amorous Quarrel* on October 24, 1658, followed by *The Blunderer* the next year and his *The Affected Young Ladies* in 1660, along with *Georges Dandin* and *The School for Wives*.

From 1795 until 1805, the Institut held its public meetings in the Salle des Cariatides until it was moved to the College des Quatre Nations on the left bank of the Seine. On the first floor, the guardroom (today the Salle La Caze) was the setting for many festivities. Sumptuous ballets were held there, and in 1601 Marie de Medicis showed off her talents in one called the *Ballet of Sixteen Ladies Representing Virtues*; in 1617, Louis XIII danced in *The Freeing of Renaud*; and Louis XIV appeared in *The Feasts of Bacchus* in 1651, *The Old Court* in 1652, *Time* in 1654, and in *The Sick Lover* in 1657. This was an outrageous display of luxury where the clothing of the princes was worth at least the price of a province. The attic above this room gave access to the Grand Degré, which was the apartment of Mazarin and his large family. The Cardinal's seven intriguing nieces were very deeply involved in court affairs, like Marie, who was Louis XIV's young lover, and who later married the Prince Colonna, or Marie-Anne, who was the Duchesse de Bouillon and protector of the good La Fontaine.

Several marriages were celebrated in the king's apartments, often together with the Salle des Cariatides, along with receptions for ambassadors, or engagements such as that of Louis XIII's sister Henriette-Marie to the King of England.

The final display of royal power was the meeting presided over by an impotent Louis XVIII, rolled in his wheelchair from the Tuileries on December 9, 1820, to mark the opening of the union of the House of Peers with that of the Deputies in the Salle des Gardes (the Salle La Caze). The following year it was changed to that as it is now. It had become another room of the museum.

The collections of paintings were kept in the king's painting room. In 1681, an inventory already included works by Corregio, Leonardo da Vinci, Giorgione, Palma Vechio, Dominiquin, Carrache, Veronese, Tintoreto, and Titian. They were shut away in "a sort of flat gilded cupboard painted on top". Engravings and drawings of the Jabach collection, bought by Colbert, as well as the collection of engravings assembled by the Abbé de Marolles were also found there. But thanks to Le Brun, the king's painting room was opened to the public in 1679.

By royal decree, an engraving workshop was created at Les Gobelins to visually record the glorious events of the reign. In a spirit of inventory, records were to be made of festivities and parades as well as monuments and works of art, and this was a precursor of the idea of an established patrimony. The collection assembled in the Louvre was the beginning of the Graphic Arts department that was founded in 1797.

The Grande Galerie also energetically participated in the activities of the court. While its lower part served as lodgings for artists, its entire first floor remained undecorated for a long time (Poussin had been approached to handle this).

Giovacchino SERANGELI. Napoleon I Receiving Deputies of the Army at the Louvre after His Coronation. *Musée National du Château de Versailles. Napoleon was very concerned with integrating the vocation of the Louvre as a museum in his policy of prestige and used it countless times as a stage for the ceremonies that punctuated his public life. When he was only a general crowned with glory upon his return from his campaigns in Italy, Bonaparte was received by the 'Conseil des Anciens' and the council of the 'Cinq-*

Cents' during a memorable dinner for seven hundred people held in the Grande Galerie. He crossed the gallery with great pomp at the time of his wedding with Marie-Louise as he went from the Tuileries to the Salon Carré, which had been transformed into a chapel for the occasion. At the time of his coronation, he received a delegation there. He closely surveyed the work undertaken at his request by Percier and Fontaine and entrusted Vivant Denon with the task of organizing the design of a grand museum.

Pierre François FONTAINE et Charles PERCIER. The Emperor and the Empress Crossing the Grande Galerie of the Museum on their Way to the Salon Carré, Transformed into a Chapel. *Musée du Louvre, Paris.*
A great many documents recount the scene. On April 2, 1810, Marie-Louise and Napoleon walked to the Salon Carré, *which had been transformed into a chapel, to receive their nuptial benediction. More than eight thousand privileged witnesses were gathered along the Grande Galerie for this diplomatically crucial moment. Napoleon made use of the space in the monarchic tradition which had made the*

Galerie des Glaces of the Château of Versailles the theatrical stage of the court. The stage for a procession that allowed the public to approach more closely its sovereign, often to petition him and make various requests and recommendations. Moments of pomp, formal conviviality and protocol.

Jean-Baptiste ISABEY. The Funeral Chapel of Louis XVIII. *Musée Carnavalet, Paris.*
In regaining the Louvre, the Restoration wanted to underline the sacred character of the monarchy. Life at Court was heavily dominated by etiquette. The display of the dead king also re-established traditions. The pomp was deliberately funereal.

Henri IV walked his dogs there, and for the amusement of the young *dauphin*, who was 5 at the time, he organized a fox hunt there as well. During the dark days of the Fronde, food was stored there and it became infested with rats. The Académie de Peinture held its first salons there (in 1699, 1704 and 1706) before moving to the Salon Carré. It ended up being a repository for relief maps of the cities of France.

In the great monarchic tradition of humility in front of the destitute, and the identification with Christ necessary to give their power credibility, monarchs touched the sick with one hand to heal them. This was the ceremony of the scrofula, dating from the middle ages, which persisted until Charles X.

On December 20, 1797, the "Conseil des Anciens" (council of elders) and that of the "Cinq Cents" (five hundred), offered Bonaparte a dinner for 700 people to celebrate his victorious return from Italy. Having changed his name to Napoléon, he organized a parade procession from the Tuileries to the Salon Carré, which had been transformed into a chapel, for his marriage to Marie-Louise. It fulfilled its initial role (of providing a discreet escape route) in 1870 when Empress Eugénie used it to flee the Tuileries Palace with Metternich, who led her right to the Salon Carré where a furtive departure ceremony took place.

While history moved on, as architects progressively enlarged the palace of the kings, constantly remodeling this ever-growing body, daily life resumed when the kings left. With Louis XIV having chosen Versailles for his residence and administrative seat, the palace was an object of desire for many. Various institutions took up residence (the Académies, the Royal Printing Press), while citizens, such as la Montespan's sister, Madame de Thianges, the Duchesse d'Estrees, the Vicomte de Polignac, and the Comte de Tesse, tried to get in, taking advantage of connections, references, or quite simply snatching up free space. The old rooms were divided and even the colonnade suffered a temporary, badly constructed compartmentalization. Cheap restaurants, innkeepers, second-hand clothes dealers and junk dealers set up shop, followed by a lively undisciplined mob. One of Louis XV's ministers noted that "the courtyards of the Louvre were the site of the most infamous prostitution and debauchery". Artists again took up residence in the unfinished parts of the Colonnade built by Le Vau. The painters Toqué, Perrin, Monnet, Prudhon, Demarne, Le Sueur, and Dufourny, the engraver Debucourt, the sculptors Houdon, Coustou, Deseines, and Boizot went there, each following his own whims without taking into account the unity of the building. The painter Jean-Louis David set up a workshop made of wooden boards in the northern section of the Colonnade.

Napoléon I drove everybody out to allow his architects Percier and Fontaine to finish the Cour Carrée and its surroundings that had already been cleared out by Gabriel and Soufflot. From this time on, the Louvre began to look the way it does today.

Jean Bruno GASSIES. Bivouac of the Garde Nationale in the Cour Carrée of the Louvre. *Musée National du Château de Versailles.*
The Louvre is married to the course of history. It is inscribed in its stones and in its pages: flamboyant, happy, solemn and at times, devastatingly picturesque. It is the hidden face of history, behind the scenes and secret.

The Symbolism of the Louvre

*T*he building of all public
monuments in the Paris
cityscape has never been without
cost. They must obey economic
and topographic imperatives, but
also have a symbolic meaning in
relation with the other
monuments around them.

Paris' vital force moves from
east to west like a call to the
horizon of the faraway sea, along
the river it was built around.

From the Place de la Nation to
La Defense there is a chain of
buildings that completes each
other, each fitting into an
admirable continuity.

The Louvre plays a capital role
in this adventure of urban
dynamism. From its early days as
a fortress at the edge of the city,
built for its defense, it became a
palace. The decision to develop it
around a square courtyard, each
side of which opens onto the city,
has maintained its impression of
being a crossroads.

When the western facade
became the main entrance, this
had to be marked by majestic
architecture. The result was
Perrault's colonnade program. It
was the best solution chosen
among several projects; Bernini's
project for this was considered to
be too Baroque and without any
real connection with the spirit of
the place. The magnificent,
slightly haughty, ample
colonnade marked the entrance
to a palace that would stretch out
from east to west.

The decision to point the
palace toward the west was
made by the position of the
Tuileries Palace, as the histories
of the two buildings always
moved in a spirit of continuity,
each one echoing the other.

At one time, the idea was advanced of placing it at the end of an avenue that began at the Hôtel de Ville, to highlight the relationship between municipal and national power.

Since then, the extension of the Louvre has been in two parallel wings, following the flow of the Seine. It included the construction of the place de la Concorde at the end of the Jardin des Tuileries, the straight line of the Champs Elysées up to the hill of the Place de l'Etoile, and, pushing farther still, the birth of the glistening steel and glass La Defense quarter, which was built is if it were a response to the great dream of the kings, engendering the modernity incarnated in their living works.

The final touch was the building of the pyramid, at the heart of the Cour Napoleon, that reinforces the singular character of this monument that is profoundly integrated in the urban fabric, and necessary to understand Paris as a coherent city in its development and balance, like a living body.

By a strange whim of fate, while Bernini's project was refused when the entrance was located at the western facade, one of his works today marks the entrance of the museum in the center of the Cour Napoleon, under Ieoh Ming Pei's glass pyramid.

Standing impatiently on its pedestal, the Louis XIV equestrian statue, placed in a

The Inverted Pyramid.
As an echo of the central Pyramid that marks the main entrance to the museum, the inverted pyramid in the middle of the shopping complex on the lower levels of the Carrousel allows light to play upon its multiple facets, like a piece of crystal. The rigorous geometric form joins with aesthetic beauty in its faces.

The Pyramid of the Louvre.
At the center of the Cour Napoleon, it replaced the two courtyards which were built during the last century. It brought a final touch of modernization so that the palace could better fulfill its mission as a museum.

position guarding the entrance, was sculpted by Bernini, even though his proposal for the Louvre had been refused. But the statue did not please Louis XIV, who sent it to the far edge of the Bassin des Suisses in Versailles. It remained there for a long time, almost forgotten. It has finally found its place, quivering with an ardor that is better appreciated today. It gives the visitor a sign of the spirit of a museum that closely links the experience of art with that of history, like the twin sisters of the human mind, in its dreams, anguish and triumph.

The Museum

*I*t was during the Enlightenment that the concept of a museum "open to educated people" made headway. Marigny, the brother of la Pompadour, did not have time to realize a dream shared by those great minds around him. D'Angiviller asked Soufflot to restore the Grande Galerie with a view to making an exhibit space. A committee, which included Hubert Robert and the sculptor Pajou, set to the task. From this ambitious program, Hubert Robert left a significant series of paintings recounting the museum, its role, and even its future "in the form of ruins."

The administration of the museum during the Directory was entrusted to a commission that included Hubert Robert, Pajou and de Wailly.

Works seized from churches and immigrants, as well as the enormous quantities of war booty captured by Bonaparte, were added to the royal collections already on the site. Now that he had become Napoleon, he highly valued the museum.

In addition to the booty from the raids made on the collections of foreign powers that he conquered and fleeced, that were brought to the museum in a procession in the ancient Roman style, from the Champ de Mars to the palace, important 'loans' were obtained from Italian towns and German principalities. This imperialist policy was lead by Vivant-Denon, a picturesque character, who wrote licentious novels, worked as a diplomat in the spirit of the old regime, and was ambitious as well as having the favor of his master. Napoléon entrusted him with the design of a Grand Louvre. When the empire fell, works that had been taken by force had to be returned. Under the Restoration, with this new situation in mind, the museum enlarged its scope more to include distant civilizations.

Until then, it had favored the Greco-Roman heritage at the origins of French culture. Archaeological adventure, which was blooming at the time, made it possible to envisage important collections containing large examples of works from these faraway worlds, while the fashion of traveling to the East, which marked the birth of Romanticism (from Byron to Renan, by way of Gerard de Nerval), developed at the same time.

In 1848, a decree officialized the creation of the Louvre in its societal purpose. "Since the provisional government considers that it suits the Republic to undertake and complete the great works of peacetime; and that the support and devotion of the people give the provisional government the strength to accomplish what the monarchy was unable to do; and that it is important to concentrate in a single and vast palace all the fruits of thought that are the splendors of a great people; does

Charles Percier. Salle de Melpomène. Musée du Louvre (Département des Arts graphiques), Paris.
Pierre Lescot's southern wing of the Louvre was doubled in 1660 by Le Vau in the vast completion project of the Cour Carrée and the eastern façade (the Colonnade). When Louis XIV abandoned the Louvre for Versailles, work was

stopped. With only the walls in place, the space remained open to the elements. It was Fontaine who took up the work again while decorating the queen's former apartments to establish an antiquities gallery parallel with the one that ran alongside the Cour Carrée. The statue of Melpomène that occupies the recess at one end gives the room its name.

hereby decree: 1: The Louvre Palace shall be completed; 2: it shall be called the Palace of the People." The museum defined itself by placing itself in the seat of monarchic power.

While the Tuileries Palace became the king's residence, the Louvre became the focus for all the cultural institutions that were to coexist with the administration.

The restoration and expansion of the Louvre no longer depended on the whims of a ruler who wanted to flaunt his power and wealth, but on an architectural logic for a palace

DROMART. View of the Salle des Antiques from the Salle de Pan.
Musée du Louvre, Paris.
Painters from the 19th century were fascinated by the museum as a subject to be painted. The aim was to fill the canvas with the museum's treasures. The Italian painter Panini's mania for accumulation can be seen here at its best.

that, finding its calling and future role, needed sufficient space to come into existence, while offering a harmonious whole that crowned its prestige.

The clearing of the unhealthy quarter remaining within the territory definitively allotted to the palace-museum (limited to the north by the rue de Rivoli) accompanied its own

The museum won out over the foreign bodies still housed in the Palace, but did so ever so slowly. Its history is that of a laborious conquest for the space it needed.

The fire in the Tuileries Palace on May 23, 1871 definitively sealed the fate of the Louvre.

In addition to the removal of one of the elements that made up its splendor (the Tuileries Palace)

implementation of conformity in accordance with its new role. The easthetic mark made by the Napoléon III style, made up of many references and pastiches, gave this development a majestic as well as a lavish look. Its pomposity, highlighted by the profusion of sculpture, caused people to describe it as a "gigantic pastry", or an "exalted confection".

François-Joseph HEIM. Charles X Distributing Awards to the Artists of the Salon in 1824. *Musée du Louvre, Paris.*
All artist careers began and were confirmed by participating in the Salon, an obligatory passage for success. Medals and orders linked the painters to the official art. Charles X was involved in the artistic life of his time. He was one of those whose solicitations transformed the Louvre into a museum.

Victor DUVAL. View of the Grande Galerie, circa 1890, after Restoration. *Musée du Louvre, Paris.*
Here the space had at last almost found its definitive form, though the picture rails were still very loaded. The 20th century introduced a new style of presentation by hanging the works on rails. By refining the hanging method and giving as much space as possible to each work, the paintings stood out, conserving their completeness and their full impact.

the Louvre Palace, partially damaged, also needed to heal its own wounds.

This was the chance for Lefuel to remodel the Flore and Marsan pavilions, as well as the Richelieu wing (along the rue de Rivoli), and for the bureaucracy to leave the museum that was nascent in those walls once and for all. The administration moved to the former Hotel d'Evreux, called the Elysée Palace.

Alphonse HIRSCH. View of the Rotunde de Mars and the Salle de Mécène around 1880. *Musée du Louvre, Paris. The rotunda was designed by Le Vau to connect the summer apartments of Anne of Austria (Petite Galerie) with those on the Cour Carrée. The decoration of the ceilings*

was confided to Charles Errard and completed in the 19th century by Jean-Simon Barthélemy with Man Shaped by Prometheus *or* The Origin of Sculpture, *when the space was designated for the exhibition of ancient sculptures. The medallions attributed to Bernard Lange*

and Jean-François Lorta and Antoine Denis Chaudet's motif (The Genie of the Arts, The Union of the Three Arts) allude to this. At that time, it was the main entrance to the museum. The Salle de Mécène was the first of the summer apartments. The ceiling is decorated with paintings by Errard and Noël Coypel. Under the Consulate, Meynier painted The Earth Receiving the Laws of Nature as Dictated by Adrien and Justinien and two grisailles: The Apian Way Restored by Trajan and The Construction of Aquaducts by Trajan.

The ministers and various institutions put up a fuss and grumbled about completely freeing the space. The Finance Ministry would be the last, and it was not until the 1981 decision to build the Grand Louvre that the museum finally took over the entire palace, and could complete the display of its treasures.

This is a huge program that is just being completed at the end of this century, after the addition of the pyramid by Ieoh Ming Pei that guided the modernist style of the undertaking.

The palace, respected for its exterior architectural appearance that shows practically a millennium of history, has been radically readapted to correspond with the rules of modern museology.

The diffusion of light (both natural and artificial), the color of the moldings, right down to the space given to people to move around, have improved the adaptation of the building, providing clearer, more dynamic presentations, whereas previously there had been a policy of overburdening the space. The museum long reflected the principle of an "amateur's painting room", of which it was a public extension with its mix of genres. The educational role of the museum and the historical discourse it illustrates require a chronological presentation written in well-defined chapters, as well as a division of genres, and a pedagogical spirit to correctly respond to the huge public it addresses. For, while the

"amateur's painting room" was limited to a small public of connoisseurs, the current museum is open to the world and should be understood by the masses. It has a primary role in making art and culture available to all.

Alexandre BRUN. The Salon Carré. *Musée du Louvre, Paris.*
The Salon Carré was a strategic place inside the Louvre, which had become a museum. Annual exhibitions organized by the Royal Academy of Painting were presented here. Starting in 1789 experiments were done in the use of overhead lighting. The most important pieces of the permanent collections were gathered here and the place was becoming a highlight for a cultured and somewhat 'mundane' society.

Giuseppe GASTIGLIONE. View of the Salon Carré. *Musée du Louvre, Paris.*
The Académie Royale de Peinture et Sculpture (Royal Academy of Painting and Sculpture) held its meetings and organized annual exhibits of its members here from 1725 to 1793, when it was dissolved and the museum opened. The Salon Carré remained the official exhibit site until 1848. In 1849 it became "the sanctuary of painting of all times and of all countries". It has seen a horde of visitors and copyists and has served as a rallying point and meeting place in front of works acting as references. The most recent transformations of 1972 adapted it to the needs of contemporary museology.

Oriental Antiquities

*B*etween the Tigris and Euphrates rivers, there are cities lost in sand. The Greeks had already made them much older than they really were. Palaces and massive walls built of brick worn down by the ardor of the sun and the intemperate forces of nature. The space grows wider and the receding horizon lends itself to reflection.

In Greece, the traveler would perch on promontories at the summit of the acropolis, conversing about lost worlds. Here was a forgotten world. It had to be imagined, reinvented from simple traces left on the ground. From a sketch, architecture had to be created with its proper volume. A few fragments giving hints of the splendors of the past and enigmatic sculptures provided enough to recreate the decor. Such as it was, such as it should be, in this land where one faced the din of clashing arms, the violence of combat and a particularly bloodthirsty spirit. Babylon is not just a dream, not just a fabulous theatrical scene.

Islam had imposed a blanket of forgetfulness. It triumphed over these lands where few witnesses saw its power. It was a marching force, a conquering force, hewing out the landscape at the point of a sword and the gallop of horses.

The ancient Orient is a melting pot of people and of civilizations, who little by little would lift their deeply sonorous voices because they had been through a dream, with echoes from the heroic pages of the Bible. This is the land of the Old Testament.

Archaeology is imbedded in millenniums and in turn, buries itself there.

Under Louis-Philippe, the site of Khorasbad was discovered under a simple pile of earth. Ancient Assyria appeared before the fascinated eyes of men. Ernest Renan, who was obsessed by the Orient, was put in charge of saving the innumerable pieces that appeared suddenly from the sands and enriched the Louvre.

Thus the beginnings of our inheritance go back in time, anchoring themselves to Sumer, Nineveh, Mari, and Ugarit, the cradle of writing.

The Stele of the Vultures.
This stele (c. 2450 B.C.), found on the site of Girsu (Tello), retains its full value as a chronicle. It represents a historical event: the battle between Lagash and Umma. It expresses itself on two levels, corresponding to two themes: the first one dealing with divinity and the sacred, and the second with the military. On the first level, Ningirsu, god of Girsu, beats the enemies trapped in a net, and on the second, Eannatum makes his army march in a tight and threatening mass. The scene is treated with a great mastery of expressive synthesis and symbolic value.

The Statuette of the Sumerian Prince.
It is the figure of Prince Di Utu (Justice of the Sun) from the old city of Uruk (today Warka), a vital center of the Sumerian civilization, linked to the Gilgamesh epic and the invention of writing. The Bible mentions it under the name of Erek. It developed and was organized in two religious centers: the temple of the goddess Inanna, wife of Anu, god of the skies who became Ishtar, and the temple of Anu, god of the skies and chief of the Mesopotamian pantheon. The religious inclination of the figure lies in the perfect harmony between power and religion, in an attitude of everlasting adoration.

On the right, Statue of Gudea.
The first evidences of Sumerian art were found on the site of Girsu (Tello), by the respective excavations of E. de Sarzec, G. Cros, H. de Genouillac and Andre Parrot. In addition to the Stele of the Vultures, numerous statues of Gudea (the Louvre owns about 15), one of the priest-kings of the dynasty, founded by Ur Bawu (2160-2145 B.C.) were found. Gudea was a great builder, always surrounded by intellectuals attached to the celebration of his policy. He identified himself with the official god of the city of Ningirsu. Under his reign, Sumerian art reached a form of classicism and a solemnity appropriate for the embodiment of the sacred function of the sovereignty. He is shown serving Enki, master of fresh waters. The celebrant holds a vase from which water springs forth. This refers to a vital problem for the population's survival, as well as a source of some of the armed conflicts with neighboring peoples.

The Statue of the Intendant.
Andre Parrot discovered the town of Mari in 1933 on the site of Tell Hariri. Mari was the capital of a dynasty (the 10th dynasty after the Flood, according to the Bible), that clashed with the forces of Lagash and Akkad, and the forces of Hammurabi, who destroyed the walls of the city. During the first excavation campaign at the temple of Ishtar, Parrot discovered among other things, the statue of the Intendant, Ebih-II, distinctive in style in its attitude of sobriety and modesty. Carved in alabaster, this figure expresses the attitude of the celebrant: chubby face, shaved head, bare torso, hands clasped on the chest, wearing a Kaunakes apron. He is the image of the typical paunchy, thickset civil servant, hanging on the sovereign's every word, as well as being a faithful worshipper.

The Passing Lion.

All the monumental splendor of the ancient Orient lies in Babylon. The city spread over more than 2 kilometers on the eastern banks of the Euphrates. Under Nebuchadnezzor, the city and its palaces grew larger, representative of his power. It was a vast complex made up of individual houses arranged side by side around courtyards. To enter the city by the Ishtar gate which passed through a set of large imposing walls, one had to follow a processional path flanked by enameled brick lion friezes. It led to the main temple adorned with the Tower of Babel, denounced in the Bible as a source of conflict among men because it challenged the heavens.

The Winged Bull.

Sargon built Dûr-Sharrukin (Khorsabad) from 713 to 710 B.C., using measurements (16,283 cubits) which had symbolic value. Seven gates in the walls gave access to the city and two palaces buttressed the fortifications. One of the palaces spread over 25 acres. The facade included a triple portal adorned with columns leading to a first courtyard giving access to the various parts of the building, each with its own function (household, military or sacred). The main courtyard adjoined the heart of the palace. The walls were decorated with sculpted, larger than life processions representing dignitaries. One could access the throne room by a triple portal whose foundations were guarded by winged bulls (front), flanked by pairs of winged bulls (profile). Animal symbolism was particularly prevalent in Mesopotamian art.

The Assurbanipal Riders.
Assurbanipal, grandson of Sennacherib, lived in Sennacherib's palace in Nineveh during his youth but wanted his own palace, which he chose to decorate with a chronicle of the city's life. Sennacherib's palace evoked the siege of Lakish (701 B.C.), mentioned in The Book of Kings *(XVIII-XX). Assurbanipal decorated his palace with hunting scenes ornamented with profuse vegetation and an elegant, regular and rhythmical script. It was of an exquisite harmony despite the innate violent temperament of this people, who were accustomed to the exhilaration of bloodshed. The decoration takes on the power while softening the violence, transforming it into an 'art de vivre'.*

Darius' Archers.
Darius I (521-485 B.C.), made Suze one of his capital cities. He built the so-called palace of Apadana, a complex structure of buildings flanking monumental courtyards with a succession of porticos and galleries richly adorned with enameled bricks and with the usual reference to lions and monumental beasts. As a warrior, Darius added lines of archers in a sober style but created a sophisticated decor which eloquently expresses the ostentatious luxury with which he liked to surround himself.

Islamic Art

*L*ike a rapid thrust anchored in the person and the example of Mohammed (who died in 632), Islam would advanced by waves of successive conquests over a part of Europe, whose history since that time has not ceased to interact with it. Every European museum must take into consideration what this civilization has brought to Western civilizations, which have been marked by changes in customs and in artwork.

In a chronological reading of the history of art, Islamic art is a part of the great Medieval odyssey. It was a shimmering tributary which came to delicately nourish a slowly developing aesthetic, while Islam itself was developing rapidly. It is important, however, to place it within its territorial significance, a neighbor of the first civilizations from which the West is a descendant. Since this art was born from the desert sun, it reflects that typical spirituality of the Middle East and its refinements born from the harshness of the environment. The deterrent nature of the forms it gave rise to, and the themes it conveys, became concrete in objects of everyday life. It was a tangible mark of a refinement which was unknown in the West of Medieval times, that were marked by the influence of the church and its sense of sin. For Islam, the real world is fragile, vain, and ephemeral. This is the main reason that one should live and savor, with greater passion its "poignant, exquisite and desirable" beauty.

Basin.
Of Syrian or Egyptian origin, this basin became the 'Baptistery of Saint Louis' because of its use during the monarchy. It was part of the royal collection and was used until 1856 for the baptism of princes. It is attributed to Ibn Zayn, with its elegant and rich decoration of alternating court characters and hunting scenes embedded in medallions, merging with the calligraphy used for the decorations where human representation was usually prohibited.

Abbas I and his Page.
Called the Grand Abbas I of the Sefevides Dynasty, Abbas I strengthened his authority over Persia and concluded diplomatic alliances with the West in order to protect himself from the Ottoman Empire. Cruel and despotic (he had his children's eyes put out) but very important to the glory of his country, he chose Ispahan as the capital city, which he had shrewdly built up. This light and gracefully constructed figure of the sovereign with his page, far from the despotic person Abbas I really was, expresses both the sweet and ambiguous character of domestic scenes in a rather idealized setting. The richness of the content greatly participates in the graphic rhythm and decorative aspects of the work.

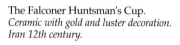

The Falconer Huntsman's Cup.
Ceramic with gold and luster decoration. Iran 12th century.

The Peacock Dish.
This dish comes from the studio of Iznik, in Turkey (mid 16th century). It is an example of the attention to detail by the miniaturist on a support which dictates its own laws. Despite the limitations, the design is loosely spread out over the surface setting off the undulating flowers which match the elegant outline of a peacock.

Egyptian Antiquities

*I*t took an ambitious little general, envied by his peers, feared by those who took advantage of his genius and his enthusiasm for the Orient, for Egyptology to become an essential branch of our knowledge of the past.

Romantic by nature, Bonaparte was also pragmatic. Politics and military campaigns to the Orient, in a spirit of conquest, were accompanied by scientists, writers, historians and archaeologists. They were the progenitors of Egyptology.

Champollion went there too. He was an exemplary figure, almost a legend, who first deciphered hieroglyphics. A civilization that had left so many monuments suddenly opened itself up to observation. With the understanding of this form of writing, everything took shape. All of the elements fit together; architecture, painting and sculpture were all closely related and collectively delivered their message.

It was just after the height of the Napoleonic era that an Egyptian Department was created in the Louvre, under the reign of Charles X who expressly designed rooms to better accommodate the vast treasures of the digs.

Through the personal efforts of Champollion, a rigorous scientific exposition was made possible by the quantity of objects in question, and the Egyptian Department became exemplary in style.

Art blends with the history of a people bearing testimony to their endurance and their relationships: from the mastaba pieced together from broken slabs to a simple cosmetic spoon and from the funerary boat to votive statuettes. This was a rich body of art completely

The Great Sphinx.
The Sphinx was an emblematic figure of Egyptian civilization. It has been multiplied and diversified, while corresponding to permanent symbolic standards: it accompanies rituals, indicates entrances and symbolizes stages. It spans an entire period of Egyptian thought with its appeal in relation to the great mysteries of the universe and its strong and thoughtful way of marking territories.

understood through its various mediums.

Egypt was, moreover, a great source of dreams, and travelers hastened to go there. The pre-eminent importance of death in such a human form, so close to daily life while attaining, at the same time, such majestic grandeur, was more fascinating than it was frightening.

Ever since the Directory, which used it for its own aesthetic model, Egypt has continued to accompany us in our dreams of grandeur and exoticism. Ramses II, Tutankaman, and Cleopatra rank among the gods in our collective memory. One meets them at every turn in the fascinating tour that the museum offers.

The Stele of the Snake King.
Djet was a monarch of the first Egyptian Dynasty (3000 - 2890 B.C.). He represents the Snake King (Ouadji), traces of whom were found in the vast necropolis of Sakkarah (a mastaba), but his tomb was more likely to have been in the site of Abydos (in Upper Egypt) where the stele was found.

The Stele of Princess Nefertiabet.
She was most likely Cheops' daughter,
which would explain why her tomb was
found in Guizeh, very close to the grand
pyramid of this Fourth Dynasty ruler.
The pyramid of Guizeh is the largest and
the most architecturally coherent site of a
sacred nature in the world. In his Book
XXXVI of Natural History, *Pliny lists*
the ancient historians who focused on
describing the site. He names Herodotus,

Diodore of Sicily and Strabon. A great
number of tombs for the queens, as well
as for the sovereigns' children, are
gathered around the great pyramids. The
stele was an integral part of Nefertiabet's
tomb. It perfectly illustrates the domestic
aspect of the environment conceived for
the long journey of the dead with its
references to food, at the same time being
elegantly represented.

The Seated Scribe (2600-2350 B.C.).
This scribe is a typical figure of Egyptian art in its majestic serenity. It is exemplary as much for the exactitude of the attitude of waiting, listening and respect, as it is for the sober, naturalist sculptural rendering that avoids exaggeration. Laid like a boundary stone on a path, the figure was caressed by the sculptor's chisel before assuming an expression of reflective submission, the modest desire to question the meaning of life before following the tranquil flow of time.

Raherka and His Wife *(2400 B.C.).*
The representation of a couple is quite frequent and associated with the idea of permanence in the face of passing time. Standing peaceful, but determined, the couple faces death with both serenity and dignity. It corresponds with this permanent feature of the Egyptian people who look at death with neither dread nor repentance.

The Amarnian Princess.
This is said to be the portrait of a princess, daughter of Amenophis IV. It dates back to the court's settling in Amarna, substituting the worship of Amon by the worship of Aton. There ensued a new Amarnian civilization, named for the site. It is one of the richest periods for Egyptian art, surrounding the legend of the haughty and mysterious figure of Nefertiti.

Fragment of a Colossus of Amenophis IV, Akhenaton.
Amenophis IV (Akhenaton) was a king of the 18th Dynasty (1379-1362 B.C.). Before moving the capital city to Amarna, he contributed greatly to the embellishment of Aton's temple. Giant sculptures surround a peristyle, where a respect for naturalism is expressed by a plausible representation of the ruler celebrating the god Aton (origin of the solar disc).

Scenes of Lamentation during a Funeral.
This was found in the tomb of the General in Chief, Horemheb. It was built in Sakkara under his supervision, after a campaign in Palestine. He succeeded Tutankamon from 1348 to 1320 B.C. The tomb's walls were adorned with bas-reliefs in the elegant Amarnian style. It is not so much gigantism as an application of style and a well mastered profusion of writing, moving to a compartmentalized narrative: it is a long processional march toward eternity which was already conceived and organized during his life by the one who is tracing the way to his destiny after death.

Amon and Tutankamon.
Succeeding Amenophis IV, Tutankamon re-established the worship of Amon as the traditional religion. In order to mark the return of the triumphing god, he multiplied the figures representative of his allegiance by placing himself directly under his protection; a hierarchy demanded by the deity and recurrent of the scene depicted. It is the symbol of the restored alliance and the emergence of royal power alongside that of the priests.

The Stele of Taperet.
Painted wood (1st century B.C.).

The Imeneminet Cartonnage.
The name cartonnage refers to the envelope composed of glued linen into which the mummy was placed and which was then laid into the first wooden coffin, which could then fit into the second coffin, according to rituals and according to the importance of the mummified

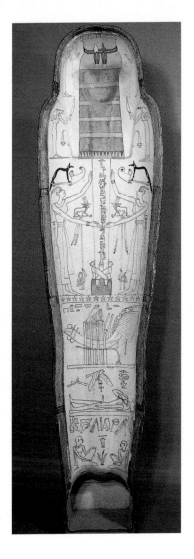

person. The cartonnage, directly in contact with the dead person, was decorated like the tomb itself, and so echoed it. Slowly deciphering these signs helped the dead to begin the initiatory journey leading them to eternity. The evocation of the god Osiris is most prevalent. He represents the god of the beyond, the mythic expression of recurrence. He was king, moon, sun, plants and the waters of the Nile. Through the universality of his powers and the symbols to which he is linked, he became the god of the dead to whom he promised a return to life or the god of passage, linked to the rhythm of life.

Bronze Cat (7th century B.C.).
The cat is an important figure in
Egyptian mythology. Considered
sacred, it is often depicted and here
represents protection in the
sanctuary. There is a surprising
realism which endows it with the
power of fascination, reinforced by
careful details such as the eyes,
which are made of rock crystal.

The God Osiris (3rd century B.C.).
The myth of Osiris begins with his murder by his
brother. He then assumed all the symbols of the
underground and of the vegetal growth he
controlled, including the mysteries of the subsoil.
Osiris, the dead king, sovereign of the life beyond
and god of vegetation, was worshipped in Upper
Egypt (in Abydos). He is therefore represented by
the double aspect of a royal mummy with the double
crown of Upper and Lower-Egypt. In his hands,
crossed on his chest, he holds distinctive signs of
power; the curved scepter (heka) and the whip
(nekheck).

Funeral Portrait *(3rd century B.C.).*
Following Egyptian funeral rituals, the
Greeks who settled in Egypt represented
their dead on the coffin. They introduced
an additional aspect by using realistic
representations of the dead having a
concern for resemblance. This resulted in
surprisingly true portraits.

Daphne Turning into a Laurel
(6th century B.C.).
Daphne was a nymph, the daughter of
the river god Peneus. As Apollo's
companion, she was, like him, a victim of
Cupid's jealousy who shot an arrow at
Apollo causing him to fall in love with
her. She, however, thwarted him, causing
him great affliction. When he tried to
approach her, she turned herself into a
laurel. Coptic art modified the meaning
when adopting it in its iconography.

Greek, Etruscan and Roman Antiquities

Loutrophore. *Terracotta. Circa 650 B.C.*
It belongs to rituals accompanying weddings
and funerals. Its decoration is marked by the
introduction of geometric figures, originating
from an "oriental style", which had widely
developed. The characters are in movement,
creating a more agile drawing, leaving behind
the geometric stiffness from which they came.

*F*rom a very early age, Western memory has been fed the booming echoes, bizarre blood baths and vituperating cries of the Homeric epic. Troy was at the heart of this belligerent and punctilious energy in the chapter concerning honor. Muscle-bound rogues and women draped in the black of eternal mourning act out Aeschylus and Sophocles for us again. The Greeks emphasized on cruelty and death as in the bloody story of the Atridae.

The emergence of Greece was accompanied by an openness to the child's world, which developed from Achilles, Hector and Ulysses and right up to the perfectly calibrated splendors of the century of Phidias who would serve as a model for us.

On the one hand was the Minotaur, and on the other, the beginnings of Athenian democracy. The birth of man, completed, marked out by objects that emerged pure of any trace of the soil from which they were conceived, celebrated and sung about in forgotten times.

It is the vocation of the museum to give meaning back to objects that are found. Greece is our womb. Renaissance man emerging from the long religiosity of the middle ages believed this and devoted all his energy to the man of reason.

Henri IV wanted to collect 'classical art' in the Louvre as evidence of the birth of modern man.

Archaeology would be the source of an impetus of curiosity which would administer the riches that burst from the soil, and design the most beautiful map possible of our past lives under the cover of a mythology that was already familiar. It invaded the arts and literature and we still live with it today.

And then came Rome, mixed up with wars of conquest and mad emperors; the temporary supremacy of the merchant over

Feminine Cyclades Head.
The basic question here is simply whether this is a fragment of a complete idol or whether it stood autonomously, the head alone being represented. The play of lines, polished surfaces and synthetic volumes are organized into a very elaborated formal syntax characteristic of a model.

99

the philosopher and of the soldier over the poet.

In keeping with its greatness, Rome would pepper its territories with grandiose monuments showing its splendor and power. It would worship borrowed gods whose names had simply been changed.

The museum has the power to engrave in eternity these relationships between man and the power of the divinities which resemble him. The antiquities are also a kind of portrait gallery of our ancestors.

The Woman of Auxerre.
Her name comes from the fact that she was discovered in the storehouses of the museum of Auxerre in 1908. Nothing was known of its origins. Its yellow-gray, fine-grained limestone dates back to 630 B.C. The gesture of the Woman of Auxerre *could be interpreted as that of worship, but it has also been seen as goddess of fertility designating parts of the body associated with her role. According to certain specialists, she could be the work of a Cretan artist.*

Head of the Rampin Horseman.
The horseman, among others, rode in the processional rites of the Panathenaea. The head in the Louvre comes from one of these cavalcades. The smile which illuminates the face is one of the specific traits of the Kouroi. It is the expression of a superabundant life which makes warriors and even the dying equals with gods. Pindare said: "We have a relationship with the gods by our body and by the grandeur of our spirit." It is the expression of "the consubstantial unity with dead children and immortals of the earth."

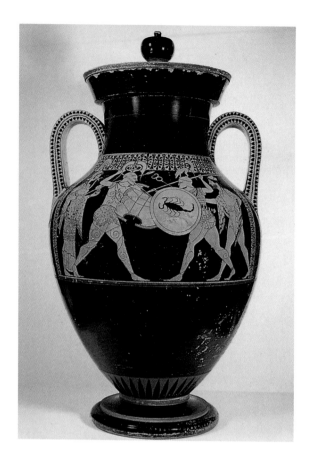

Amphore of Andokides.
Instead of being used to create the figures as silhouettes, the varnish is used as a background and it is the figures which stand out, emphasizing the color of the clay. This was a revolutionary procedure that allowed the artist greater freedom of graphic expression. It was with the associates of Andocides that this important reversal of values occurred. Similar to sculptured figures, and coming from the same enumerative principal, the scenes ornament the sides of the amphora at its widest section. There is a contrast between the battle scene and the music competition; two activities which were part of the education of a Greek in the name of the necessary balance between that which was physical and that which was intellectual.

Apollo of Piombino.
An impression of perfect life emanates from works of this period (around 480 B.C.): "at the same time animal and divine, carnal and spiritual, revealed and secret, which alternate uninterruptedly and incorruptibly in the faces and bodies". One has this same feeling of harmonious development of the species, of respect and of tenderness when considering the beaming form of Apollo of Piombino. It is a perfect testimony to the great Triumphal Odes.

The March of Ergastines (*a frieze from the Parthenon*).
The program of decoration of the Parthenon displays all of Grecian genius at its apotheosis. It was planned over a long period of time and created in close collaboration with Pericles. It entered into the political and religious view of social order. It is coherent in its conception, mixing myths with civic duty, materializing knowledge and worship in the midst of a population surrounded by this mythological poetry. Renan exclaimed in the excitement of this discovery: "Oh, what nobility, what simple and true beauty!". Art, here, attains the essentials to which it aspires: the world, life, and to give the best, that which deserves to be perpetuated.

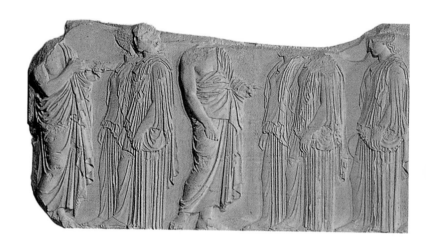

The Winged Victory of Samothrace.
An emblematic figure of art at its moment of perfection, the Winged Victory of Samothrace *got its name from the place where it was found. An important religious complex dedicated to the gods was situated there. This sculpture was conceived relatively late (190 B.C.). Its distinguishing feature is its dominant forward thrust, like that of a figurehead of a ship. We can deduce that* it celebrated a maritime victory. It was erected at a dominant point on a site, as it is today a majestic figure at one of the main entrances to the museum. The admirable series of folds which envelop the body and which reveal it furtively is both an homage to feminine beauty and a sort of poem to the wind which sculpts nature, vivifies the body, and participates in a kind of vast symphony of the elements in a deified carnal blaze.

The Venus de Milo.
In the majestic view, that the museum composed for it in a rigid framework soberly paved in marble, it presents itself as the emblem of femininity and grace. Discovered in 1820 on the Island of Melos, she was identified as the representation of Aphrodite. While her gesture remains an enigma, despite numerous hypotheses, her missing arm, according to many admirers, plays an important role in the static force that she emanates. This is proof that it is less important to be realistic than to give a significant meaning or a satisfying form from reality. Like the Mona Lisa, with which this sculpture shares popularity in the Louvre, the Venus de Milo is a work which establishes itself by the enigma it retains and the discreet mystery with which it is permeated.

Borghese Gladiator.
Greek statuaries offer numerous examples of figures in movement. This civilization, which had invented the Olympics and celebrated the serene force of the body in sports, favored art which glorified strength and which made the body play in all its muscular beauty. In the Borghese Gladiator is distilled the beauty of anatomy in an idea of force in movement, even though the objective is not revealed here since the figure is deprived of its accessories.

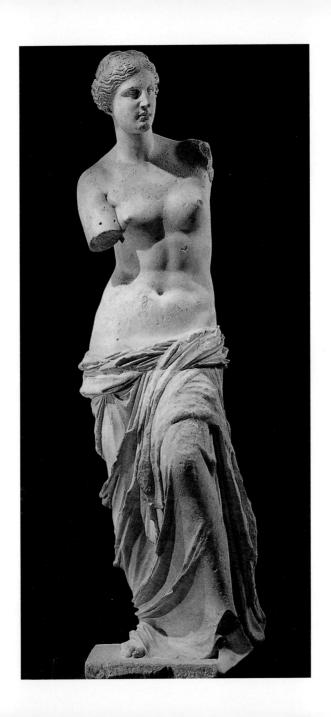

Campana Plaques.
The pronounced taste for decoration in Cretan architecture led to an intense production of painted elements made on plaques of terra cotta that were either fixed onto walls or used to decorate tombs.

The type of figures chosen correspond to conventional norms. It was a simple figurative language, repeated and developed on friezes, giving emphasis to geometric figures which frame and give rhythm to the narrative sections.

The Sarcophagus of the Reclining Couple.
One of the specific traits of Etruscan funeral art is the transposition of gestures from the world of the living to the place of the dead. There is a familiarity of tone, a

kind serenity which is a real challenge to death and a hymn to life. In using the familiar position of a banquet, the celebration of a festive existence is made, associating the couple "between the bed and the table".

Mural from the Villa of Publius Fannius Synistor.
The painted decor of the villa of Publius Fannius Synistor, located on the hills of Vesuvius (today the village of Boscoreale), is, along with the Villa of Mysteries (in Pompeii), one of the most famous. It gives an extremely useful indication of the objectives of wall painting and of its progress. Far from being only a painted image on a wall, with a strictly decorative goal, these figures give the impression of advancing "in front of the wall, like people in movement". It is a captivating verism, which animates all the available surfaces and populates the house.

Marcellus by Cleomenes.
Greek statues were used as examples of minutely realistic portraits, with attention given to resemblance. So it was for a sculpture by Cleomenes, the Athenian (who died in 23 B.C.), to produce the portrait of Marcellus, son-in-law of Augustus, married to Augustus' daughter Julia. Recognizing the implicit Greek superiority in this area, it is an opportunity to identify characters ranging from persons of public life to Olympic gods. This representation was useful for political purposes.

Jupiter of Dalheim.
This work got its name from the place where it was found in 1863 (Dalheim, Luxembourg). In its territorial expansion, Rome carried with it models like that of Jupiter from the Villa of Hadrien. The one from Dalheim also has the same broad and dominant body language.

Hadrien.
Although its objective was only to express restraint and a certain majesty, the bust portrait of Hadrien made him more human. One can see more clearly the personality of the model. Hadrien himself was tall and had an elegant manner, which is expressed well by this bust. His face is surrounded by short, thick, curly hair and a soft beard. He expresses a soft spirituality, and this is a reflection of his complex and refined personality. The bust, found in Crete, bears the mark of the Hellenistic tradition. Roman art was modified as it moved away from its center, marrying with local trends and offering a successful synthesis.

The Judgment of Paris *(mosaic from Antioch).*
This is a late mosaic (2nd century AD). It shows the perfection that was attained by a technique widely employed in decoration and which voluntarily used mythological themes. Here is the confrontation between Paris, the Trojan shepherd-prince, and three beautiful women of Greek mythology: Athena, Hera and Aphrodite, in what was the first stage and origin of what would become the Battle of Troy. The decoration surrounding the story consists of a profusion of vegetation punctuated with portraits and studded with birds.

Objets d'art

*T*he Objets d'Art Department continues the tradition of the collector's studio as it was known during the 17th and 18th centuries. It is a picturesque and skillful mixture where the object carries new significance.

As opposed to ecological museums, popular arts and traditions, this department does not aim at the social and historic reproduction of the object, but at promoting its aesthetic quality. The archaeology departments promote a general understanding of the civilizations they represent (Oriental antiquities, Egyptology), but the art object department is more artistic and recognizes the craftsman's talent, invention, and aesthetic effort. This sustains a certain seductive ambiguity, for it explains how artistic sense has entered into man's everyday life and how a useful object can also be artistic. It might be an elegant pouring vessel or a tiny statue. Any shape of even modest dimensions extends man's gestures by a certain measure.

The Objets d'Art Department inherited the items of the French Crown's furniture repository, which was housed in what is now the Naval Ministry building (at the Place de la Concorde). One can find furniture, vases and bronzes as well as precious stones. It is the expression and the display of a quality of life which used to be the exclusive privilege of the Court and certain rich people.

A succession of purchases and gifts have enriched this already extensive collection providing an overview of almost all periods as a chronological anthology. The collection on display, which expresses the splendor of the social life at that time, also includes historical evidence (the *scepter of Charles V*, the *shield of Charles IX*, the *mace of the Ordre du Saint-Esprit*, *Anne of Austria's jewelry box*, the *crown of Louis XV*, *Empress Eugenie's tiara*). Some pieces of furniture find their place naturally. Cabinetry is also a very important form of artistic expression; a prestigious and a powerful economic lever that the Louvre takes into account.

Equestrian Statue of Charlemagne. *This was among the treasures of the cathedral of Metz. Alexandre Lenoir acquired it in his campaign to preserve works threatened by the Revolution. It is an important piece in the iconographic research of the Carolingian monarch.*

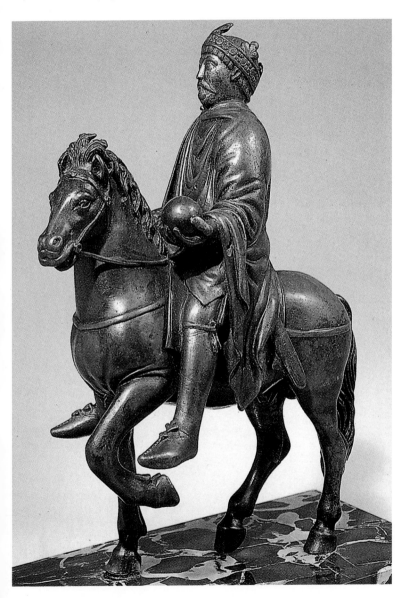

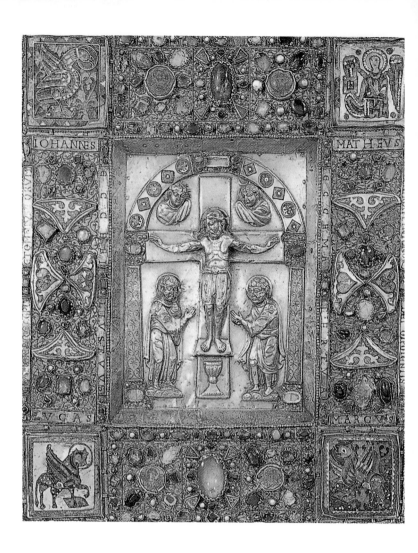

Fine Bookbinding. Crucifix of Béatrice de Trèves.

There exists a great tradition of richly ornamented bookbindings (here with gold, cloisonné enameling and precious stones on wood). The inscription identifies the person for whom it was destined, Beatrix, daughter of Frédéric II de Lorraine, who married Boniface de Toscane, later Geoffroy Le Barbu, Duke of Lower Lorraine and of Brabant. By its style and richness, this piece can be attributed to the work of Othonian goldsmiths.

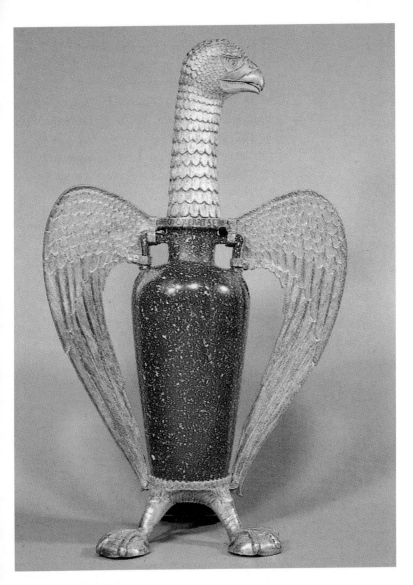

The Eagle of Abbot Suger.
Suger, an abbot at Saint-Denis, found this admirable porphyritic vase of either Egyptian origin or that of imperial Rome. It was his idea to place this vase in a gold framework evoking an eagle. "The ensemble gives the impression of power mixed with superiority shown by the rigid wings, the natural position of the talons on the prey and the proud head with its ferocious eye."

The Virgin and Child of the Sainte-Chapelle.

This belonged to the treasure of the Sainte-Chapelle in 1279 and was endowed by Charles V with a set of jewelry containing precious stones which has disappeared since. Charles V, like his brother the Duc de Berry, was greatly attracted to work in ivory. His collection includes ancient and commissioned works. The "ymagiers" (sculptors of ivory) worked for the Court, as did the "couteliers" (cutlers) or the "tabletiers" (fancy turners) who furnished mirrors, combs, engravings, knives, writing tablets and chess pieces. The "mestier d'entaillerie" or "tailleur de menues oeuvres" designates sculptors specialized in very small pieces.

The Virgin and Child of Jeanne
d'Evreux.
*Jeanne d'Evreux, wife of Charles IV le
Bel, the last direct descendent of the
Capetians, was a benefactress to the
abbey at Saint-Denis. In 1339, she gave a
reliquary containing small relics from the
Sainte-Chapelle, two statuettes, a gold*
Saint John *and this* Virgin and Child.
*A masterpiece of Medieval art, this
statuette is distinctive because of the
technical perfection and style with which
few works of the period can compare. It is
placed on an enamel base which retraces
the episodes in the childhood of Christ
and of the Passion.*

Polyptych Reliquary of Floreffe.
*This polyptych got its name from the
place where it was conserved until 1825,
the abbey of Floreffe in the Meuse. It is
representative of goldsmiths' work from
the second half of the 13th century
influenced by Gothic art and its
statuaries with striking lines, expressive
angles and filled with great and solemn
softness.*

Self-portrait of Fouquet.
This is what remains of the ornamentation of a diptych that Etienne Chevalier, secretary and advisor to King Charles VII, commissioned for Notre-Dame-de-Melun. The Virgin there, as the legend goes, had the features of Agnes Sorel. This is the first self-portrait of a French painter, who studied in Bourges in the tradition of the Limbourg brothers, and who would become the first painter to introduce the spirit of the Renaissance to France after a voyage to Italy.

Scepter of Charles V (called the Scepter of Charlemagne).
Charles V confided this scepter to the abbey of Saint-Denis on the night before his death in preparation for the crowning of Charles VI. The reference to Charlemagne, propagated by the Valois who were coming to the throne, was justified by the concern to reinforce a legitimacy that was being threatened. Similarity with the name (Karolus) reinforced it. The scepter was used for all coronations for the kings of France after 1380, except for that of Charles VII and Henri IV. It was present even at the coronation of Napoleon but only as a simple reminder. Finally, it was used at the coronation of Charles X, the last king to be crowned.

The Plate of Isabelle d'Este.
This is the work of Nicolo da Urbino (1520-1545) from whom Isabelle d'Este, Marquise de Mantoue, had commissioned a set of plates decorated with her family's coat of arms. It was inspired by a subject from the Bible, Abimelech spying on Isaac and Rachel, *and frescoes of Rafael in the Vatican loggia. From them came a strict style reserving large spaces for action.*

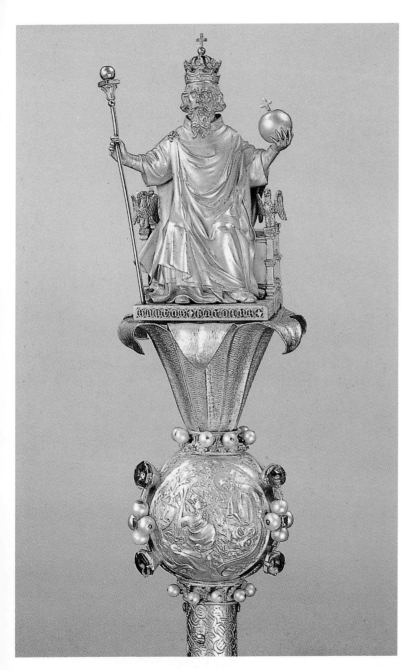

Crown of Louis XV.
This was created by a jeweler, Augustin Duflos, from a design by Claude Rondé for the coronation of Louis XV in the cathedral of Reims on October 25, 1722. It is the only one which remains from the ancien régime. The richness of its ornamentation makes it the most sumptuous example known. Among the 282 diamonds which ornament it are the Regent and the Sancy, today replaced by copies, and 64 colored stones (16 rubies, 16 sapphires and 16 emeralds).

Léonard L<small>IMOSIN</small>. Portrait of Anne de Montmorency.
In 1545, the artist was commissioned by the king to do a series entitled The Twelve Apostles. *He became the valet and enamalist of the king. He used a technique that was traditionally associated with the decoration of objects of worship and inspired by biblical history for new cultural inspiration where mythology reigned. In addition to decorating numerous domestic objects, he began painting portraits. The style that was abrupt and stiff, "northern", in the enamel technique, softened with him, becoming more Italian in style. His works are the most abundant and the richest in variety, bearing decorative motifs that framed the portraits. These constitute the gallery that best represents the society of his time.*

Allegory of Water.
This is in the tradition of the Fontainebleau school, which often referred to the theme of water, giving it all of the grace and mystery of mythological legends. It is directly inspired by the vignettes of Raphaël Sadeler, which were created on the theme of the Four Seasons. It is surrounded by a poem by Guillaume de Bartas entitled The Creation of the World.

Altar from La Bastie d'Urfé.
This comes from La Bastie d'Urfé (Loire) and is rich in detail. In it one sees all of the fantasies inspired by the grotesques discovered in the Golden House of Nero in Rome. The decoration of the earthenware plaques shows the development of the art of gardening as a continuation of the functions between the outside and the inside of a dwelling. It introduces nature into the home and the meticulousness of a refined life into the garden. It is the decoration of an altar step dismantled in the 19th century.

Charles CRESSENT. **Chest of Drawers.**
This is the major work of Charles Cressent (1685-1768). It is ornamented with gilded bronze motifs: cherubs, acanthus leaves, ivy and lion's claws. There is quite an admirable decorative expression scattered along the soft and comfortable curve of the piece, which has two drawers that are well integrated into it.

André-Charles BOULLE. **Armoire.**
André-Charles Boulle (1642-1732) worked for the court of Louis XIV and he combined the rigor of solemn and monumental forms with a complex veneer, where figures made from shells and golden metal fittings combine. This is a decorative profusion that is admirably controlled, preserving the practical character of the piece of furniture and giving it an impressive majesty.

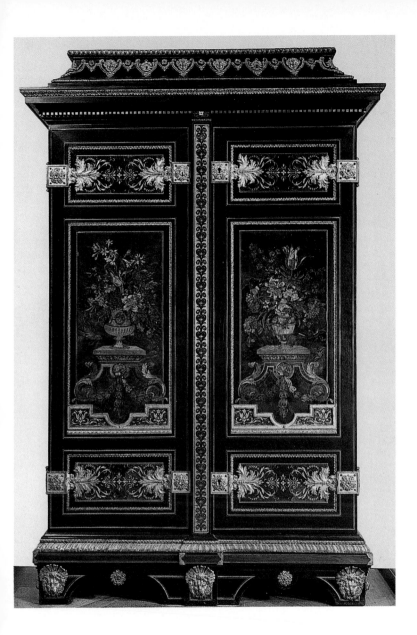

Sculptures

*T*his department was created relatively late. The sculptures which were in the Louvre were only the "leftovers" of a number of unfinished works which were never displayed, such as the *Rotonde des Valois*, due to go to the Saint-Denis basilica, or the *Illustrious Frenchmen* destined to adorn the Grande Galerie. Lastly, the Royal Academy of Painting and Sculpture located in the Louvre, began storing "received objects". However, well before it became a museum, the Louvre had started collecting classical art. When it was created, it became the aesthetic ideal in that it embodied the revolutionary spirit heralded by the painter David. With a curious and significant exception, Michelangelo's Slaves entered the Louvre's collection in 1974. But hadn't Michelangelo himself, in his youth, tried to pass off one of his sculptures as a piece of classical art?

At the closing of the Museum of French Monuments that Alexandre Lenoir had created at the Petits-Augustins convent (today's Ecole des Beaux Arts),

part of his collection went to the Louvre, adding the Medieval and Renaissance sculpture collections it was lacking up to that point. A purchasing policy promoting Medieval art, vigorously led by the Marquis de Laborde, followed by Louis Courajod, met with the hostility of the governing bodies that exclusively preferred classical art. The department finally won its autonomy with great difficulty.

The final aspect of the Louvre's acquisition policy confirms the ever greater concern to preserve "outdoor" works from pollution. Some of its most beautiful sculptures were thus moved from the Jardin des Tuileries in order to protect them. Recently, the *Marly Horses*, which framed the entrance to the Champs-Elysées, were also placed into the courtyard to which they have given their name. This has become one of the strengths of the sculpture department, because by respecting the monumentality of the exposed works they are displayed to their best advantage. This is also one of the new aims of the museum.

Saint Michael Slaying the Dragon.
12th century.
This came from the Benedictine abbey in Nevers where it decorated the tympanum of a chapel dedicated to Saint Michael. Within the limits permitted by this type of work, the sculptor knew how to give a great expression of strength to the figure of Saint Michael in an excessive dramatization, while squeezing together the two figures in a sober and efficient design with an amply decorative effect.

King Childebert. *13th century.*
This is a sculpture of the founder of
the abbey of Sainte-Croix-Saint-
Vincent, which became Saint-
Germain-des-Prés. It decorated the
entrance to the abbey's refectory.

Charles V. *1365-1380.*
It is thought that this statue, along
with the one of Jeanne de Bourbon,
decorated the entrance to the Louvre
at the time of work undertaken by
the king for its embellishment. It
passed into the collections of
Alexandre Lenoir in the Museum of
French Monuments (1796) and
then to Saint-Denis before
returning to the Louvre in 1904. It
is particularly remarkable for the
realistic expression, the desire to
represent the psychological presence
and the physical strength of a king
who was known for his intelligent
indulgence and his lucid
benevolence, despite his
unattractive appearance. A real
dignity and an exemplary spiritual
grandeur emanate from it.

Tomb of Philippe Pot.
This tomb comes from the abbey church of Citeaux (late 15th century). The dynamic creative center of the 'Etats de Bourgogne' is joined with the expressive vehemence of primitive Flemish works. Religious fervor gives it a solemn dramatization which highlights a style full of accents and strange inflections. There is a movement from the traditional recumbent effigy to a theatricalization of the funeral cortege with its monumental mourners.

Donatello. Virgin and Child.
15th century.
A major figure in Italian sculpture, Donatello moved from the stiff sculpture, commonly expressed by Gothic art, to the radiant harmony of lively Renaissance figures. He practiced all styles, worked on numerous sites, and constantly renewed his skills. Vasari noted: "He left so many works around the world, that one could rightly affirm that no other artist worked as much as he." He tried all kinds of techniques: from flat planes to the round, in marble, bronze or wood. He knew how to create an admirably airy and well-proportioned space in a bas-relief. From a recurrent motif, he made a lively, unique composition where fervor is balanced with elegance.

Pierre BONTEMPS. Charles de Maigny. *16th century.*
Trained by Rosso, and a collaborator of Le Primatice for casting in the method of classical works, Bontemps also worked with Cellini. Even though his roots were in the spirit of the Fontainebleau school, he did not limit himself to using a style which was ultimately foreign to him. A certain harshness of temperament and a serious, rustic character turned him away from it. He specialized more in funeral sculptures where he knew how to harmonize the true character of the figures with a decor of elegant sobriety. He worked on the tomb of François I at Saint-Denis. He chose to represent Charles de Maigny in a posture full of life and calm strength. This work was to be placed in the Eglise des Célestins in Paris.

Bust of Louise de Savoie. *Ca. 1520. Unknown in France, except for their vocation in reliquaries, bust portraits were particularly popular in Italy in the great tradition of antiquity. But far from restricting himself to marble, a noble material, artists did not hesitate to use terra cotta. The source of resemblance gives it documental value. This one of Louise de Savoie, the imperious mother of François I, is part of a group which decorated the facade of the Château de la Péraudière (in Touraine).*

Barthélemy PRIEUR. **Funerary Spirit.**
The Funerary Spirit *is part of the tomb
of Christophe de Thou, the first president
of the parliament of Paris, who died in
1582. It is part of a tomb monument with
several figures. Placed below the bust of
the deceased, framed by Virtues in bas-
relief, are two naked spirits in bronze.
Their knowledgeable and suave attitude*

*owes much to the Michelangelo in the
Chapelle des Medicis. This work differs
from conventional models by a calm
sensuality and a body contour which
shudders with a powerful life to the point
of expressing the extreme affliction
demanded by the role played by the entire
composition.*

Germain PILON. **Suffering Virgin.**
*The brilliant career of Germain Pilon is
associated with the favor he had with
Catherine de Medicis in the plan to edify a
monumental mausoleum to the memory of
Henri II. Germain Pilon had already
worked on a project for the tomb of François
I that was never finished. For the tomb of
Henri II, Catherine de Medicis first ordered
the central monument destined for the
Couvent des Célestins. It is the silent round
of the Three Graces. For the more ambitious
project of the Rotonde des Valois at the
basilica of Saint-Denis, Germain Pilon
worked with Le Primatice. We
attribute to him the two Cardinal Virtues*

*in bronze and four bas-reliefs which were
images of the deceased. Dressed and in
prayer, nudes and recumbent effigies in an
admirable palpitation of flesh. The*
Suffering Virgin, *which accompanies a
Saint Francis in Ecstasy and a
Resurrection, was also planned for this
composite group. The* Suffering Virgin
*was inspired by existing models, but here
Pilon removed the body of Christ, giving
the attitude of the Virgin all the intensity of
pain she appears to be enveloped in. In the
end, the work would be placed in the church
of Saint-Paul Saint-Louis in Paris. The
terra cotta in the Louvre is simply a study
for the final work.*

Antoine COYSEVOX. Renown Mounted on Pegasus. *Late 17th century.*
This work was originally planned for the sculptural decoration of the Parc de Marly where Louis XIV liked to go in private company. Its counterpart was Mercury Mounted on Pegasus. *The work went from Marly to the Tuileries gardens in 1719. The horseshoe-shaped entrance to the garden was designed to accentuate the swing bridge. The groups by Coustou and the two Renommées of Coysevox were brought from Marly to the Tuilerie gardens. It was in 1986 that it was again moved to the Louvre to ensure its protection.*

Pierre PUGET. Milo of Crotona.
In the style of Bernin, Puget transposes the rhythms and the breath of painting into three dimensions. One sees him treat the caryatid with ample vehemence at the Hôtel de Ville of Toulon, at the same time that those of Jean Goujon or even those of Sarrazin in the Louvre are part of the tradition of sculpture applied to architecture. In the Milo of Crotona, Puget attains an expressive vehemence and the sensual and tragic twisting of a Rubens showing a palpitation of the flesh in suffering. He allows waves of muscles, taken to their extreme limits, to run along the body.

139

Nicolas COUSTOU. Adonis Resting after the Hunt. *Together with his uncle Coysevox, Nicolas Coustou received commissions in 1707 for three statues along a bucolic theme destined for the Parc de Marly.* The Hunter *(also called* Adonis Resting after the Hunt *in accordance with the mythological fashion) is a robust work. For a long time it figured in the sculptural decor of the Tuileries (where Coustou was largely represented), decorating the terrace of the château. In 1870, it was added to the collections of the Louvre.*

René FRÉMIN. The Companion of Diana.
René Frémin worked for the Granja Park in Spain, in a style close to that of Marly, where the theme of Diane (and her companions) was favored. This is part of a tradition of gallantry and reverence for lively women and is dedicated to the rites of the hunt, which structured the social life of the court. Here one sees great liberty of tone, vivacity in design and joy with a touch of outlandishness. The enveloping of her body gives her rhythm as well as petulance; it clothes the body less than it celebrates her grace.

Edme BOUCHARDON.
Cupid Cutting His Bow
from the Club of
Hercules. *1750.*
The large Fountain of the
Seasons *in the rue de
Grenelle, where the sculptor
uses baroque style rhythms
and classical order, is well
known. In* Cupid Cutting
His Bow from the Club
of Hercules, *he uses
movement and reaches
toward a grace which
announces a looser
sculpture. The piece did not
receive the recognition of
the Court it was destined
for, and was removed from
the Salon d'Hercule in the
château of Versailles and
sent to the Choisy property.*

Jacques-Augustin PAJOU. Psyche
Abandoned. *1790.*
*This piece matched the Cupid by
Bouchardon but it did not please the
Court because of its realism. It was too
solemn, causing the figure to move from
its mythological realm to a much too
familiar reality that the Court refused. It
demanded instead that art idealize life*

*with epics and myth. Despite this, Pajou
produced a charming, slightly
melancholic nude which inspired Pierre
Julien, who created* Amalthée *(or* The
Goat Suckling the Young Girl*), which
decorates the dairy of Rambouillet. One is
led from classical-baroque styles to a
graceful and more human iconography.*

CNIDIE PERDITE PUDICA

143

144

Jean-Antoine HOUDON. Sabine Houdon. 1793.
Houdon is not only the creator of Voltaire Sitting, which imposed a certain image of the writer, but he is also responsible for a series of delicate portraits of exquisite sobriety of craftsmanship and powerful observation. More than anyone else, he knew how to capture the furtive tenderness and mischievousness of childhood, here with his own child.

Antoine CANOVA. Psyche Revived by the Kiss of Cupid. 1787.
The celebrated sculptor, who was Napoleon's favorite, refined lines and slimmed volumes until reaching a style valued for the boldness of its flight of fancy, tangles, the complexity of its arrangements and a search for a precarious balance. Based on an ancient legend, it here reaches an exceptional mastery. The piece was acquired by Murat. Canova abundantly supplied works to Napoleon's entourage.

James PRADIER. Satyr and Bacchante.
*This work was not well accepted when it
was presented in 1834 : "The pose is of a
lascivious nature so common that the entire
grouping, instead of presenting a
voluptuous picture which was so admired
by the Ancients, rather disgusts us by the
indecency of the lines and of the effect". A
journalist expressed the common opinion by
saying that the work was "vile, disgusting
and miserable". Pradier is credited with*

*participating in a great movement of reform
of sculpture in the 30s when there was a
separation from classicism. While
remaining faithful to mythological themes, a
more natural, shameless and observant
version removed the body from its literary
conventions to give it its own life. What
passed for indecent was a simple refusal of
truth; to see the body in its reality was an
insult to the ideal of beauty.*

François RUDE. Young Neapolitan
Fisherman Playing with a Turtle. *1833.
Although he received a classical education,
François Rude is considered to be a
representative of romantic sculpture. He
used this style with heroic patriotism in his
most famous work* The Departure of the

Volunteers *at the Arc de Triomphe. His*
Young Fisherman *comes from a happier
inspiration and a more familiar realism. He
attempts to grasp a spontaneous expression
and a fact of life without falling into the
picturesque.*

Paintings

While a true lover of artistic works loves to surround himself with the most refined creations of his time, François I, the promoter of important sites like the château of Fontainebleau, was also conscious that his political position was enhanced and his prestige increased by drawing on art. A tradition developed and many monarchs would strive to develop projects and collect art works. At the same time as he had the Louvre enlarged, Henri IV gathered together classical art works. With Louis XIV, despite the transfer of the Court to Versailles, the Louvre and its royal collections developed and were enriched. It was this already large collection which would constitute the foundations upon which the Convention, at the time of the Revolution, would create the museum. Added to the royal collection, were the collections of the Academy and the works seized in the homes of emigrants and confiscated, like the belongings of the Church.

Napoleon enriched this museum by plundering, abusive loans and seizures of war booty, to fill this museum under the enlightened direction of Vivant-Denon. It was this universalistic vision which the Louvre continued, through its shrewd policy of buying works of art, the opportunities for donations and more recently for payments in kind, which have thankfully filled in gaps.

In its beginnings, the museum had what was largely a pedagogical role. It had days when it was open to copyists and a few days open to the public. Since then, there was an increased demand by the public with a decrease in the number of copyists, to a relentless few. They present an added attraction since many are fascinated by the possibility of transferring these masterpieces, that capture our attention and nourish our memory, onto canvas.

For a long time, visiting the Louvre was the best school for painters who came to find the secret of their art. Chagall confessed that upon arrival in Paris he went there quickly "because here was the truth. Here it was serious." Miro, also immediately after arrival in Paris, went to the Louvre: "I wanted to see all of the paintings." Giacometti declared: "I have almost all of the Louvre in my head, room by room, painting by painting."

The creation of the Musée d'Orsay, which took the works from 1848 to the first years of the 20th century, unburdened the presentation of the Louvre of its many collections from the 19th century. At the same time, the transformation of new rooms (in the Richelieu wing) permitted works which had been unavailable to the public to be brought out of the repositories.

With its different tours (French school and foreign schools), the museum today offers an exceptional anthology of the history of western painting. This completes a remarkable collection of sketches from all schools, alternately presented with the painting galleries along the tour route. This is a background which permits temporary expositions to be organized and offers researchers a gold mine of resources.

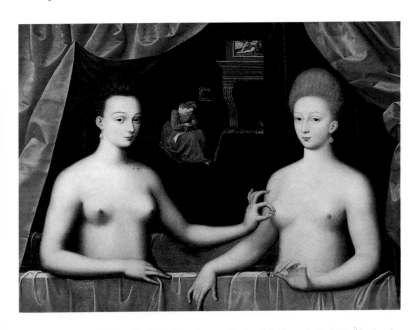

Fontainebleau School. Gabrielle d'Estrée and One of her Sisters. *Late 16th century. Italian influence can be clearly seen in the works produced by the Fontainebleau School through the whims of the king (François I) who made art an instrument of his prestige. He was the first to use it whereas, up until this time, it had almost exclusively been in the service of the Church. This led to a noticeable change in the subjects treated; they could be* gallant and, in the context of this refined and subtle Court, were exclusively of women. Ordinarily, like poetry, they were compared with the prestige of mythological examples that they echoed. In this delicately impertinent composition, one can see the domestic nature of the scene, which is reinforced by the servant in the background who is preparing garments as in the compositions of Titian.

Georges de LA TOUR. **The Sharper.**
Ca. 1630.
The arrangement of the characters around a table is technique that was used whenever a painting touched on profane subjects and penetrated into the daily life of the people it portrayed. Here, emphasis is given to luxurious garments and a certain stiffness of the expressions, corresponding to the plot to swindle a naive player out of his money. By insisting on the position of the hands, the gestures and the way the subjects' eyes meet, the painter composes a striking, frozen comedy in a sumptuous material with a masterfully presented story.

Nicolas POUSSIN. **Winter** (*or* **The Flood**). *1660-1664.*
This work is part of the series, the Seasons, where the painter summarizes, in one scene, the richness and the diversity of the ingredients that make up a moment in natural life (light, human activity and atmosphere). For Winter *he chose the tragedy of the Flood, which is quite removed from his way of having serenity spread over all of nature. In an atmosphere which announces the great climactic effects of Romanticism, he risks using large and dramatic gestures. This presents a quite surprising aspect of his own genius; he in whom classicism is incarnated.*

Claude GELLÉE (called LE LORRAIN). **Ulysses Returning Chryseis to His Father.** *1644.*
Le Lorrain loved ample composition and gave particular attention to decor where architecture played a preponderant role. He was generally inspired by existing monuments, thereby offering a sort of anthology of portions of architecture. He took various places and joined them together in an "ideal" landscape.

Louis Le Nain. Peasant Family in a Home. *1640.*
In a rather rich series of works inspired by the peasants' world, this is his most ample, monumental and ambitious painting, as can be seen by the number of characters in the scene. More than just a meal, the painting shows the resting of the family around the food and the rite which brings them together around the table, with a child musician who becomes the center of the action. By the posture, the faces and a certain quiet

heaviness of their attitudes, the work shows peasant life in all of its difficulty and nobility, giving it a timeless dimension. In the reflective and solemn pages of his diary, Charles du Bos stated: "The haggard and ardent beauty of certain faces, and especially the brownish, round form from which these faces seem to have appeared in one stroke. The child seated at the far right of the painting is unforgettable. It is the same pathetic child, but more austere, as the one from The Sick Child *by Metsu."*

Philippe de Champaigne. The Ex-Voto of 1662.
Highly favored by the Court, Philippe de Champaigne got closer to the circle of Port-Royal around 1646 through the intermediary of Arnaud d'Andilly. He sent his two daughters to board there in 1648 and painted numerous canvasses for the community (a Communion, *a* Saint Benoît, *a* Good Shepherd *and a* Saint

John the Baptist*). As thanks for the healing of one of his daughters, he painted this* Ex Voto *of 1662 showing nuns who were part of the congregation. Champaigne is, here, in perfect accord with the spirit of those who commissioned his works. By nature, he had a tendency for austerity and spiritual contemplation. It was in works connected with Port-Royal that he gave the best of himself.*

Page 153 :
Charles LE BRUN. Chancellor Séguier.
This work shows the arrival of the
Chancellor in Rouen just after having
put down a revolt (1640). At the time of
the inventory of 1793, the commissioners
noted "the great mastery, the magnificent
order and the strong male touch of this
great master". One might guess that the
representation with pomp and ceremony
of the Chancellor surrounded by his
officers had a political purpose, since
Séguier had to defend his position in the
face of competition born out of what
followed the Fronde. For others, the
painting represents the Chancellor at the
time of ceremonies organized in honor of
the august infant Marie-Thérèse when
she entered Paris (1660).

Jean-Antoine WATTEAU. Embarkation
for Cythera. 1717.
The survival of a young spirit in a body
altered by illness softened Watteau's
thinking and inspired a work marked by
both infinite tenderness and deep sadness.
He imagined tender and voluptuous
scenes, ballets of fine ladies and
gentlemen in shimmering silk and satin
plunged into a crepuscular world. The
landscape of the Embarkation dissolves
in the distant lands announced as a
promise. The island is inaccessible, only a
fantasy or a simple dream.

François BOUCHER. The Luncheon.
1739.
Very much in favor with the Court and
with the nobles for whom he was
working, Boucher received orders for
decorative construction sites in castles
and houses. He adorned them with

pleasant and sensual scenes from
mythology or everyday life, thus making
a reputation for himself. He also knew
how to set the tone for scenes from daily
life, as seen here with an intimate and
tenderly familial note, giving real
testimonies about the society of his time.

Jean-Baptiste GREUZE.
The Punished Son. *1778.*
*In contrast with the avowed
debauchery Boucher's painting
glorified (who was favored by the
court and painted sprightly scenes
for rich clients), Greuze's attitude,
supported by Diderot, featured
morality in painting, representing
the civic virtues of all stages of
family life.* The Punished Son *is
comparable to other paintings
which refer to a chronicle of life
with its highlights and emotion-
filled moments. This is expressed
with large but controlled theater-
like body language.*

Jean-Marc NATTIER. Countess Tessin.
1741.
*In the incomparable pleiad of portrait
painters of the 18th century, Nattier
made a name for himself by passing
through the house of Orleans, where he
was the favorite painter. Introduced to
the Court at Versailles, he received
commissions for portraits for the
entourage of the king. Similar to Rigaud
by the sumptuousness of his palette, he is
more intimist, giving his models a
softness of expression forbidden in official
portraits. He painted less the dignity, the
role or the social prestige of his subjects,
and more a certain humanity of each of
his characters, locked in a privileged but
structured world, that could not always
escape the agony of melancholy. He gives
this woman a vision which announced
the world of Jean-Jacques Rousseau, one
where convictions would waver and
which would draw nearer to natural
values.*

Jean-Siméon CHARDIN. The Olive Jar.
1760.
*By specializing in still lifes, Chardin
learned to give them a new and unique
dimension. Ordinarily, the still life is a
display of objects that is sometimes
marked by an awareness of the vanity of
all things (which gives the name
"vanités", used forsome of them).
Chardin on the other hand, concentrated
on the profound and silent life of the
object. He searched for the essence of life
in all things. The quality of light,
caressing, shining and rich, reinforces the
impression of capturing the object in its
entirety and in its essential true nature.
He painted less the symbolic than the
expression of the objects, a choice which
was eminently modern.*

Jean-Honoré *FRAGONARD*. Portrait of
Madeleine Guimard. *1768.*
*Every work of Fragonard is centered
around femininity. La Guimard was one
of those who commissioned his work for
her hotel in the Chaussée d'Antin. In her
portrait, Fragonard deployed all the
vivacity of his style: pleasant and alert,
heady and at the limit of impertinence.
He liked attitudes that were liberated
from all constraints, the sudden
appearance of the body in space, and
twists, which give the body in its best
light and emphasize its natural grace.
Each woman is in movement with broad
gestures. Their charm comes more from
the vivacity of their behavior than from
their features. He wanted his painting to
be in the movement of life.*

Jacques-Louis DAVID. Portrait of
Madame Récamier. *1800.*
*Together with his "heroic" works inspired
by great literary texts or y revolutionary
events, David was a unique and attentive
portrait painter. He voluntarily deleted
the superfluous details of the
surroundings, capturing his subject in a
bare space, giving all the attention he
desired to human presence. A simple
concession was made in the case of
Madame Récamier, that is the famous
chair she gave her name to, around which
her sitting room in l'Abbaye-aux-Bois
was organized. The flirtatiousness of the
model is mixed with the rigor of vision in
the ethical logic of the artist, who
expounded the rules of classicism, using it
in a modern and Spartan way. The style
makes reference to classical art.*

Théodore GÉRICAULT. The Raft of the Medusa.
1819.
*The painter was inspired by a news report, which
created a scandal since it resulted from the
deficiencies and complacency of authorities who
gave responsibility of the frigate Méduse to an
incompetent captain. The shipwreck resulted in the
death of the majority of its passengers. Those who
managed to climb onto the raft experienced a
terrible ordeal where most of them perished and
were eaten by those who survived. Géricault shows
here his fascination with death, and one can see
putrefying corpses. He actually worked on the
anatomic details after having observed the dying at
the hospital Beaujon, not far from where he had
established his studio.*

Jean-Dominique INGRÈS. The Turkish
Bath. *1865.*
The Turkish Bath *is the last in a long series
of bathers and odalisques which are the
centerpieces of the work of Ingrès. It betrays
one constant which is his fascination for a
voluptuous and feminized Orient. He finally
had the opportunity in 1865 to conceive a
work, which was audacious at that time,
commissioned by a Turkish ambassador
residing in Paris. His imagination was
nourished by reading relevant material, such
as the famous letters of Lady Mary Wortley
Montagu. He began the work after having
done many studies. It remained confidential,
in the possession of the person who
commissioned it. At the time of that person's
death, it was put on the public market and*
*began its true career. Théophile Gautier was
lyrically enthusiastic, but the Goncourts,
reacting in their Journal, spoke of a
"mingling of mannequin-like bodies being
disproportionate like a caricature; a group of
savages from the "Land of Fire", cut out of
spice bread...". This aggressiveness persisted
until the beginning of the 20th century, with,
for example, the comment by Paul Claudel,
who spoke of "a canvas of the miserable
painter called Ingrès, which is called* The
Turkish Bath, *where one sees a mass of
women packed together one against the other
like a cake of maggots". On the other hand,
Jean Cocteau recalled the dying Marcel
Proust, contemplating this work for the last
time with satisfaction.*

Eugène DELACROIX. Liberty Leading the People. *1831.*
It was Delacroix' revolutionary enthusiasm which allowed him to take advantage of the "Trois glorieuses" which put an end to the evil regime of Charles X. He had already given proof of his ideas favorable to liberty in The Massacres at Chios *which celebrated the Greek insurrection. The work was disliked and criticized at its presentation at the Salon. Henri Heine found the characters to have 'expressions like jurors' and it is declared that this work is generally an apologia for the rabble. The composition is meticulously done and every detail has a coded meaning. The presence of the Notre-Dame cathedral in the scene recalls Victor Hugo's famous work honoring it. The presence of Gavroche symbolized a similarity in their way of thinking and social choices which united the two.*

Camille COROT. The Lady in Blue. *1874.*
Famous and appreciated primarily for the incomparable subtlety and the grace of his landscapes, Corot was also dedicated to feminine figures which presented a more intimate and relatively confidential aspect of his character. This is one of his last canvasses (1874). It is distinctive by the delightful and tender lighting, and the bareness of the surrounding environment which highlights the serene and elegant presence. The dress, which gives the painting its name, is a true pleasure for the artist; a steady execution, realism without embellishment, frankness which testifies to an exceptional certainty, and complete mastery of his faculties at a time when the "trembling" of his landscapes lead him to needless repetition and opened the way for imitations which he accepted with indulgence and a natural benevolence.

FRA ANGELICO. **The Virgin's Crowning.**
Ca. 1430.
This was painted for the San Domenico altar in Fiesole. Vasari described it with enthusiasm. It has been in the Louvre since 1812, following the abrogation of monastic life at the time of the Napoleonic campaigns. Though the predella has been a source of discord and was perhaps painted by students, the principal panel is the painter's masterpiece. He attained a pure style with both a precision in detail and a monumentality that superbly convey the sacredness of the event. A joyful and innocent communicative ardor emanates from the painting.

Andrea MANTEGNA. **The Ordeal** *or* **Saint Sebastian.** *Ca. 1480.*
For a long time this work was kept in a church in Aigueperse, a small village in Auvergne. It had been brought there by Claire de Gonzaque (the daughter of Frédéric, the marquis de Mantoue and the person who commissioned it from Mantegna) at the time of her wedding with Gilbert de Bourbon-Montpensier. In addition to the religious theme, the painter composed an anthology of architectural references, creating a kind of stone art museum in the foreground and a dream landscape in the distance. There is an abundance of details and a concern for exactitude which characterized the archeological mania of the first Renaissance. "It is my painting," stated Vieira da Silva. "I can not dream of the Louvre without thinking of it. The shades of gray in the bodies... This image is very sharp. The archer is a Roman portrait and the design is tense, intense and sharp. Look at how the arrows are made. A great hidden force. One can't be harder or deafer than that arrow. A pianist has to have great strength to play without sound."

165

Lorenzo BOTTICELLI. Venus and the
Graces Offering Presents to a Young
Girl. *1470-1480.*
*It was in the highly cultural refined
climate of the Court of the Médicis that
Botticelli made his debut. He painted his
famous* Allegory of Spring *and* Birth of
Venus *while there. These are recurrent
themes along with variations on the
themes of love and birth. He evoked, in a
fresh and childish way, a certain image of
women; fluid and airy, slender and
innocent.*

Leonardo DA VINCI. The Mona Lisa.
1503-1506.
*The fame of this work has led it to be copied
by caricaturists, and this has partially
weakened its mystery. Even so, it is a
summary of the intellectual abilities of
Leonardo da Vinci and of his approach to
his figures; always giving them a strange,
soft and enigmatic light.* The Mona Lisa
*is true enigma. Questions have been asked
as to the identity of the model, even to go
so far as to suggest that it was a young
man. Credit was finally given to the
woman who inspired it, Mona Lisa, the
wife of Francesco del Giocondo a
Florentine notable. The smile and the
position of the hands have also resulted in
considerable speculation concerning the
painting. It is a work typical of the artist
who loved wild distant lands, misty
landscapes and a vaguely worrisome
fantasy world. In contemplating the
figure, one forgets the surrounding
environment. This perhaps contains
answers to some of the questions. It is in
contrast with the apparent calm. It can be
compared with another work by Leonardo
da Vinci,* The Virgin, the Child and
Saint Anne. The Mona Lisa *was
acquired by François I, and during his
time was exhibited in the Bains wing of
the château of Fontainebleau.*

RAPHAËL. Saint George. *Ca. 1504.*
This subject was repeated several times by the painter. This version was painted for Henry II of England, who Guidobaldo de Montefeltro wanted to thank for having decorated him with the Ordre de la Jarretière (Saint George being the patron saint). The figure here is clearly separated from the light, airy landscaped background. The monster appears suddenly in all its aggressive strength. Saint George's angelic nature shows that he will be the winner.

Antonio CORREGGIO. Jupiter and Antiope. *Ca. 1526.*
Between two great decorative projects (the frescos of the dome of San Giovanni, Parma, and the cathedral of Parma), Correggio devoted himself to paintings (1524-1526). In this painting the rhythm is animated, the lines are lithe and the play of light is soft and mobile. Correggio heralded the audacity of baroque art with the open sensuality that he presented through the pretext of mythology (Venus, Satyr and Cupid). This work was part of the collection of Louis XIV.

TITIAN. The Concert. *Ca. 1510.*
There was, for a long time, great
hesitation to attribute this work to either
Giorgione or Titian, until finally it was
recognized as a work of the latter. It was
part of the collection of Jabach where it is
mentioned, along with a work by
Giorgione, as decorating the apartment of
the Duc d'Antin during the French
Regency. It passed through Versailles
before entering the Louvre in 1792. The
subtle beauty of this work comes from the
evocation of music as a unifying force of
body and soul. One can note how it
differs from a work by Correggio who "in
looking to present the transparency and
color of the flesh with colored shadows,
moved away from an ideal conception of
complexion" as used by Titian. Perhaps
it speaks of a moment of inner peace in
the Garden of Eden.

CARAVAGGIO. Death of the Virgin. *1606.*
This work was painted before Caravaggio
committed the murder that made him a
fugitive. It was commissioned to decorate
the chapel of Santo Maria della Scala in
Trastevere, but was refused because the
virgin was not painted with enough
dignity. The work was recovered for the
Duc de Mantoue by Rubens, who acted
as negotiator. It was part of the collection
of Charles I of England, then that of the
banker, Jabach, who sold it to Louis XIV
for the decoration of Versailles in 1671.
From there it entered the revolutionary
Museum in 1793.

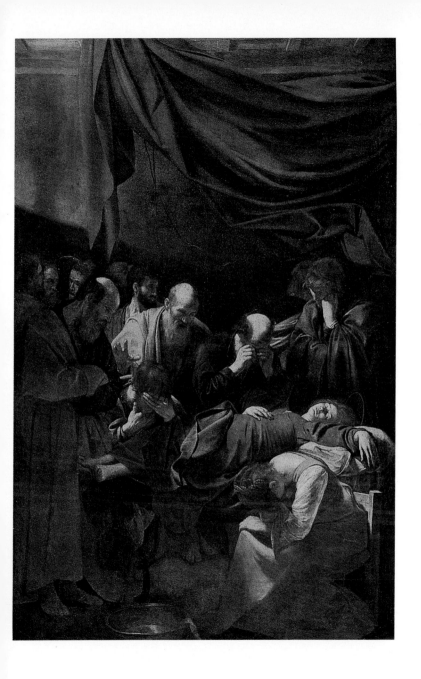

Jan VAN DYCK. Madonna with Chancellor Rolin. *Ca. 1435.*

Nicolas Rolin, born in Autun, was chancellor of Burgundy and Brabant. He created the Hospice de Beaune and commissioned Roger van der Weyden to paint The Last Judgment, *in which he is also represented. Several proposals were made for the city in the background: Maastricht, Liege, Utrecht, Lyon, Geneva and even Autun were suggested. "While contemplating these vast but tiny cityscapes, where hardly recognizable characters come and go in public courtyards, though precisely painted to accomplish with exactitude everyday tasks, one may ask whether the painter's thoughts didn't join those of the astrologer or mystic, and if his intention was not to insert a painted universe in God's world, endlessly echoing its measures..."*

Hiëronymus BOSCH. The Ship of Fools. *Ca. 1494.*

This was the first time that this painter treated the theme of "an attitude essentially critical and morale in opposition with human foolishness which neglects the teachings of Christ". He was inspired by the work of Sebastian Brant: Das Narrenschiff *presented in Bale in 1494, and* The Ship of Fools' *by Badius of Ghent which appeared in Paris four years later. The work is also exceptional in that it is the "oldest panel created using a technique of extraordinary brilliance where strong composition, that can be seen sometimes through thin pictorial layers, depicts the figures by a few brush strokes or suggestive impastos".*

Pieter BRUEGHEL (The Elder).
The Beggars. 1568.
This works has many interpretations. One
may see: a list of human vanities, different
social classes (king, bishop, soldier, burghers
and peasants) and clearly there is a group of
lepers, the symbol of degradation and of the
sins of humanity. "As we know him,

Brueghel appears as one of the incarnations
of solid, common sense that flourished in
western Europe during that century along
with others like Erasmus, Thomas More and
Rabelais. He is an example of common sense,
but in his own way since he was a
philosopher descended from generations of
peasants".

Jacob JORDAENS. The Four Evangelists. *1624.*
From his collaboration with Rubens (as his first assistant, who participated directly in the composition of the 21 paintings commissioned by Marie de Médicis for the Luxembourg palace that can be seen today in the Louvre), Jordaens conserved a taste for a generous, ample, vibrant and savory technique. The Four Evangelists (1624) is a pure baroque masterpiece with the idealization of the characters in an animated group,

and with realism seen in the facial details as well as the natural, powerful expressions. All is in movement, power is magnificently dominated. Even if he was reluctant about the artist, Paul Claudel didn't hesitate to praise the work as the best that the painter had ever accomplished. He particularly noted the central figure of Saint John: "I don't know if human art has shown us a figure more holy, more filled with authority and virile fervor than this friend of Jesus in his youthful austerity."

Peter Paul RUBENS. Hélène Fourment.
Ca. 1640.
*There are numerous portraits of Helen Fourment,
the wife of the painter; alone, with her children, in
his company and taking a walk. Rubens
consecrated his art to his young wife with a
liberty of tones, a joviality and a discreet
tenderness which presents a more personal aspect
of the man covered with honors and familiar with
the Courts. Louis Hourticq commented that "by
the affectionate softness, the warmth of love and a
peaceful atmosphere of joy and goodness, he
shows that, for this artist, strong and at the peak
of his glory for whom life was a triumph, almost
without a struggle, nothing like the sight of his
happy loved ones penetrated his soul with such
profound happiness. Nothing like it made his art
glow with such a light, moving smile".*

REMBRANDT. Bathsheba Bathing.
1654.
*The artist made his Bathsheba
impressively large. In this domestic
scene, he gave attention to the heavy
embroidered fabric, "rolling like a
wave" and the ceremonial lighting
which gives it a sense of mystery and
of waiting. Designated by destiny,
Bathsheba prepares for it with
uncertain seriousness. The faraway
lesson from Venice and its brilliance,
is marked by deep sadness.*

VERMEER. The Lacemaker. *Ca. 1665.*
Exceptional and fascinating, the work of
Vermeer sparked numerous commentaries
and held the attention of writers who saw
in it a moment of perfection. Paul Claudel
spoke of "blazon colors" and points out the
clarity of the light which surrounds these

beings and their gestures as if to tear them
out of their temporal reality. Here is a pure
expression, "pared down, sterilized and
cleansed of anything material" according
to the same Paul Claudel who finds in it "a
mathematical candor".

Pieter DE HOOCH. An Interior, with a
Woman Drinking with Two Men, and
Maidservant. *1658.*
*If the use of space is characteristic of
Vermeer, here it is treated in a radically
different way. This work is more anecdotal
and sensitive to savory details observed in
social situations, presenting them in a*
*friendly and relaxed manner. In a sparsely
decorated background, the painter finds
the eloquence of Franz Hals. Where
Vermeer would use a soft and soothing
light, Pieter de Hooch plays with direct
lighting which enlarges the room,
throwing down heavy shadows giving the
scene captivating realism.*

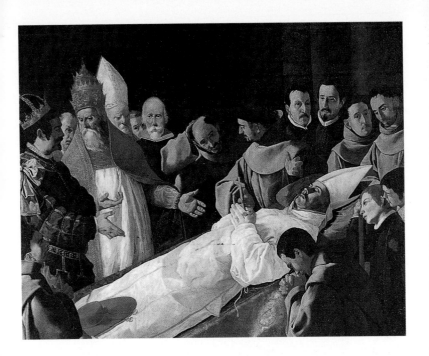

Francisco ZURBARAN. The Lying-in-State of St. Bonaventura. *Ca. 1629.*
The painter was commissioned to paint six large canvasses to decorate the church of the Franciscan school San Buenaventura de Sevilla. In the end, he only did four of them, two of which are in the Louvre. The Lying-in-State *is the most remarkable. There is a striking contrast between the figure praying in the foreground wearing a habit, nervously and dramatically pleated, and the figure of the saint, stiffened by death in his light-colored alb which lightens the entire work. The circle of praying figures, having a great variety of attitudes and expressions, confers a mysterious solemnity.*

EL GRECO. Crucifixion with Donors. *Ca. 1580.*
Contemporary of Saint Louis, King of France. *Framed by the ostentatious piety of the donors, Christ is in a position of peaceful majesty which contrasts with the turbulent state of the cloudy sky, filled with strange and tormented light. The painter moves the drama of the crucifixion toward its surroundings, giving the body of Christ the delicate contours of an immaculate body.*

Jusepe DE RIBERA. The Clubfooted Boy.
1642.
Ribera's taste for "dark compositions with violent lighting effects were seen in his early works" but The Clubfooted Boy *is a late work (1642). He moved toward a technique using more light, large movements, and a sense of the picturesque, where sparks of sensuality* *would alternate with realism. This is a work done in the Spanish tradition of observing misery, or art at the street level. The painting belonged to the king of Naples, where Ribera spent most of his career. It was given to France in 1802 to compensate for damage done to the church Saint-Louis-des-Français by Neopolitan troops.*

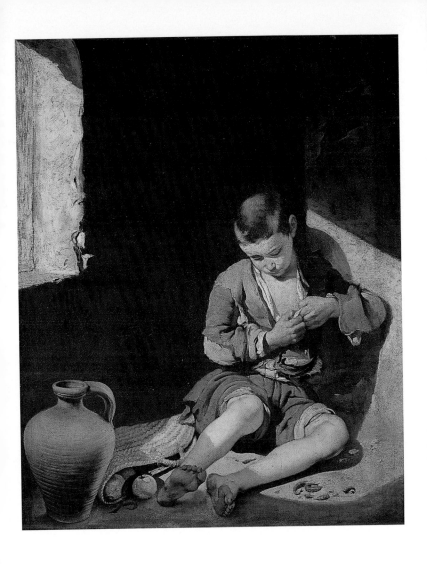

Bartolomé Esteban MURILLO. The Young
Beggar. *Ca. 1645.*
*This was an early work by the painter
(1645). It was acquired for Louis XVI by
the art dealer, Le Brun. As a painter of
children, certain critics state that*

*"Murillo is the Spanish Titian or Rubens.
It seems that he studied children carefully
because he remembered, from the
profusion of carefree models that
Andalusia offered him, their way of life
and their charm."*

Francisco GOYA. The Marquesa de la
Solana.
*This work, dating from the period 1794-1795,
was part of a long line of portraits in which
Goya knew how to give a personal touch,
while at the same time using admirable shades
of black, giving the model an expression of
modesty and dignity. "What a marvel,"
exclaimed Giacometti, "is done with the least
possible means, it has as little color as
Mantegna yet it is dazzling." It is a simple
work where the law of painting imposes its
norms, spreads out its riches and defines a
space where a certain intensity vibrates. It is a
presence which goes beyond the simple
personality of the model but instead captures a
thought which burns from the interior.*

Francisco GOYA.
Ferdinand Guillemardet. *1798.*
*The model was ambassador from France
to Madrid in 1789. Goya took into
consideration the conventional portrait
style but shattered the haughty and
solemn character of official portraits by
giving this figure a life-like appearance.
He captured him in an informal position
with vivacious movement. The official
quality is given by the sash, which adds
bright colors to the dark uniform, and the
hat on the table, which repeats the
pattern in a tangle of feathers.*

Albrecht DÜRER. Self-portrait. 1493.
Of his various self-portraits, this is the first
with any significance. It was preceded by a
sketch he did in 1484 (at the age of thirteen),
one from 1491, one on the back of The Holy
Family and lastly a self-portrait from the
same year as the one in the Louvre. It was a
sort of preamble to a finely developed work
which shows the man in the splendor of
youth. It was destined for Agnès Frey, the
painter's fiancé. This explains the thistles in
his hand (a "symbol of marital
faithfulness)". Dürer was 22 at the time.
Goethe greatly admired this painting because
"everything in this work was done with
excellence, with perfect, meticulous care and
a harmony of details".

Hans HOLBEIN. Portrait of Erasmus. 1523. Helbein completed two portraits of Erasmus, this one being destined for Thomas More. It was given to Louis XIII by Charles I in exchange for a work by Leonardo de Vinci, St. John the Baptist. *It has been thought that the quality of observation and psychological strength came from a close relationship between the painter and his model. If Holbein and Erasmus had been friends, the latter did not really realize Holbein's importance. He considered him a simple artisan, and carried Dürer to the summit of the hierarchy dominated by the humanistic spirit. Holbein didn't have the knowledge of Dürer but, nevertheless, "thanks to his artist's eye, assimilated the laws of style, elegant lines and techniques of form, just as they had been developed by the Italian Renaissance".*

Lucas CRANACH. Venus. *1530.*
It was by the instigation of Jean de Constant that Cranach went from religious representations to feminine figures inspired from mythology. Here, he remained faithful to his caustic style, to strange inflections, to mannerisms greatly underlined by the incongruity of the hat in relation to an acerbic nudity.

Caspar-David FRIEDRICH. The Tree of Crows. *Ca. 1822.*
Between the sea and the mountains, the painter constructs a space where nature exalts its mysterious forces. It is a transposition of the impulses of a tormented soul, since, for the artist "the conception of nature is not subject to either literal description or the idealization of living things. Natural motifs are considered like the hieroglyphics of divine revelation". Acquainted with poets, a friend of Ludwig Tieck and one of the great figures of German Romanticism, he was inspired by places he knew well (the Island of Rugen and the banks of the Baltic Sea).

Thomas LAWRENCE. Portrait of John Angerstein's Children. *1808.*
Being precocious, he confronted Reynolds' glory at
a young age and appeared to be a rival to be feared.
He knew how to render physiognomy with rare
dexterity, a touch of elegance and a quiet charm
which would bring him great fame. He became the
most sought after portrait painter of his time.
Everyone who posed for him, and often with the
whole family, revealed the tone of an England that
was distinguished, bucolic and already romantic.

Thomas GAINSBOROUGH.
Lady Alston. *1760-1765.*
Gainsborough was a portrait
painter in vogue with the
aristocracy. He was able to reconcile
many things in his work: the